SCIENTIFIC THEORY OF GOD
PROOF THAT GOD EXISTS

by

JOHN MICHAEL THOMPSON

D1553573

Published by
Brighton Publishing LLC
501 W. Ray Road
Suite 4
Chandler, Arizona 85225

SCIENTIFIC THEORY OF GOD
Proof that God Exists

by

JOHN MICHAEL THOMPSON

PUBLISHED BY
BRIGHTON PUBLISHING LLC
501 W. RAY ROAD
SUITE 4
CHANDLER, ARIZONA 85225
BRIGHTONPUBLISHING.COM

COPYRIGHT © 2012

ISBN 13: 978-1-62183-127-3
ISBN 10: 1-621-83127-2

PRINTED IN THE UNITED STATES OF AMERICA

FIRST EDITION

COVER DESIGN: TOM RODRIGUEZ

DEDICATION

To my wife, Mae

*Whose belief and support
made this book possible*

Scientific Theory of God: Proof that God Exists ~ John Michael Thompson

TABLE OF CONTENTS

INTRODUCTION

O ur scientists say there is no evidence that God exists. They say there is no need for God, because evolution and the big bang explain how we are here. The purpose of this book is to show where science has gone wrong and to scientifically prove that God does exist.

Mortality is the most important issue we humans will ever face. Science rules modern life and teaches that we human beings are insignificant animals lost on a minor planet among billions of planets, suns, and galaxies in a seemingly infinite system of material objects. Scientists believe they have investigated the whole universe and conclude there is no evidence of anything for us beyond the reality we are now experiencing.

Modern science has been so influential in recent times that what they teach is now considered common sense, and anyone who questions the modern scientific model is considered as being contrary to accepted beliefs and out of the mainstream. People don't understand why anyone would even seriously question the modern scientific world-view. In today's culture, believing in a Supreme Being is mostly considered quaint or out of touch with reality. The scientific minded consider belief in God as something associated with the "unenlightened."

We do not want to just die and disappear, however, so many of us manage to have faith in God despite science. Some of us search for meaning in some other way. Many others have accepted their fate and pretend that they can have a meaningful life without God and heaven. The younger generation is being brought up in a culture dominated by science, so they don't understand anything other than today's scientific picture of reality. Millions of people are living only for the here and now in what they perceive to be a godless and meaningless universe.

Unfortunately, we put too much faith in science, because it is a false impression that scientists understand the universe and how it exists. Modern scientists are trained to observe and measure the physical world that we humans see around us, and they are good at it. Modern scientists and engineers have discovered how objects interact in space and time, which has led to the invention of our wonderful modern material world. But there is a downside, because the modern scientific method teaches scientists to be strictly objective and not consider anything as real except things that can be observed and measured.

If only objects exist, then objects can only be explained by more but smaller objects. How is it possible for objects to always be made of objects? This restricted way of thinking makes it impossible for scientists to ever understand how the universe ultimately exists, because believing in only what can be sensed and measured leads to the dead-end physics of nothing but objects all the way down to nothing. This limited thinking has produced something out of nothing theories, such as string theory, the standard model, and the Big Bang. The latter supposes that the whole universe was once a hot, dense glob of plasma smaller than an atom. These modern scientific theories do not answer the ultimate question of how things exist in the first place. Scientists are searching for a smallest building block thing, but if it were to exist, how could it be made of nothing?

At some point in their explanation of things, scientists must explain where physical things come from in the first place. All they are able to say is that objects simply do exist, and everything we see just somehow came into existence out of nothing. The problem with this answer is, even though scientists have written books about it, they cannot scientifically explain how something can actually come from nothing.

What is not fully realized by scientists and the general public alike is that something from nothing is like a magician pulling a rabbit out of a hat. Science should not be based on magic.

So despite what scientists claim, they do not know what matter is, they do not know how the universe exists, and they do not know whether or not God had or has anything to do with it. It is time for modern science to look beyond the physically detectible object world in order to scientifically understand the universe and how it does in fact exist.

Something from nothing is magic, but physical from nonphysical is not. We would all agree that unobservable nonphysical things like thoughts do in fact exist. There is more to the universe than what we can see. That's what this book is about: extending science beyond our seen world into the unseen nonphysical world in order to understand the true origins of the universe.

This book connects our scientifically observable world to the scientifically unobservable realm of God and souls. This book solves the scientific mystery of how objects exist, which in turn proves that God does in fact exist. For the first time in modern history, science and God are united in one world-view. This book is not about religion or how people worship God. This new scientific world-view will revolutionize your concept of the universe, your concept of

God, and your concept of your journey in this life and into the next. It is a book unlike any you have ever read.

When I told people that I was researching this subject, they wondered why I would waste my time. To me this total acceptance of modern science shows just how serious and far gone the problem is. The fact that people have so completely bought into what they think is a godless universe is why I believe there is no other subject as crucial to human survival.

Like most people, I used to think scientists know everything about how the universe works, so I believed them when they said there is no evidence of God or heaven, but I still wanted to know for myself. I had quite an awakening when I found out that scientists don't even know what the universe is made of, let alone whether or not God made it. This is why I am writing this book: to show that scientists are not the experts on God that they claim to be, to correct the scientific model of the universe, and to scientifically prove that God did create our universe.

Before we get started I want to say that I am not a scientist; I am an engineer. I look at things from a different perspective than an established scientist would. My expertise is in designing things, systems of things, and the operation of systems. I am amazed that I find myself living in this wonderful world, which is the biggest physical system of all. I have never taken my life for granted, which has led me to a lifelong passion to understand the universe and my place in it. My career has helped me immensely in this regard. This book is about that quest.

If you read this book, you will believe in God.

CHAPTER ONE

Life in the Modern World

L ife in the modern world is mysterious. What is this place in which I find myself living? Am I a special being created by God at the focus of the universe, or am I no more than an insignificant person (animal) living on a remote planet lost in space and time? Religion is how a person worships God, but religion cannot prove God actually exists. Religion requires intuition and blind faith. Scientific discovery is the only method humanity has that is capable of proving in fact whether or not God exists.

It is true that scientists have examined the universe and claim God does not exist, because they say there is no evidence to support God. But an inability to find evidence of something does not disprove something. The problem is that scientists haven't yet figured out how the universe really works. Even scientists will admit that they don't have a clue as to what the material world (matter) is made of or how it exists in the first place, so their claims about God are not

1

credible. Until scientists can explain what matter is and how it exists, they really do not yet understand how the universe exists or whether or not God is responsible. Something is wrong with the modern scientific model, or it would be able to answer the universe's most fundamental questions.

Unfortunately, today's scientists do not publish their shortcomings, and so people are not aware of the confused state of today's science. Scientists talk as if they do know how the universe works, and therefore people trust science too much. Popular scientific opinion is causing the majority of the world's population to unnecessarily disbelieve in God.

Over twenty-five hundred years ago in ancient Greece, Thales, the first Western philosopher-mathematician, realized that we could not really understand the physical world without first understanding what physical things are made of. And here we are, well into the twenty-first century, with scientists still unable to explain what things are made of or how the universe exists. No scientist in history has ever been able to explain what matter is or how it exists. They say it just somehow is here—but that is magic, not science. The secret of matter is the biggest and most important mystery in all of science. This book will show that it is the key to understanding the universe and having unquestioned belief in God.

The truth is that scientists have been very successful at understanding the interactions of objects in nature through the development of Newtonian (classical) physics, the theory of relativity, and quantum mechanics, all of which have given scientists and engineers the power to convert nature's elements into the modern world. None of these scientific developments, however, has shed any light on what makes up the so-called fundamental particles. Today's scientific theories formulate how objects interact, but they do not formulate what objects are or what they are made of. Scientists continue to search for but have never found a smallest object of which everything else is made. A smallest indivisible object cannot be made of anything itself. Sounds impossible, doesn't it?

Modern scientists overlook their inability to explain how the universe stands alone when they say the universe is not dependent on a creator. Just because something is very small compared to us doesn't mean you can ignore how it came to exist in the first place. It is not enough to say particles simply exist.

It is confusing to live life in today's world. You may start life being told about God and Heaven, but then you go to school and are taught that God does not exist. You are told that scientists can explain everything and there is no need for a creator God. Religious leaders say God does exist, but you must rely on faith. Yet it is hard to have one hundred percent faith when you think the scientific evidence proves a different picture.

Today's world is founded on the tremendous success of scientists discovering how objects interact, which has led to all the wonderful products that make our lives easier. It is not surprising, then, that people believe the scientific version of reality. This success gives people the false belief that scientists know how to explain the entire universe and its processes. Even a very religious person usually has some doubts about God in the back of his or her mind.

Most people trust science, but they also don't want the natural world to be all there is. People don't want to just fade away into nothing, so they hedge their bets with God. Then again, they think it would be foolish to believe something that is not true. If there is a God and heaven, then you and everything you do has meaning, and you would be wise to think about and plan for the future here and beyond. If there is no God, then you and the things you do have no meaning whatsoever, and you may as well live for the present and do what you want. You would live life differently if you knew for sure how the universe really works.

People who do manage to intuitively achieve unquestioning belief in God, providence, and heaven see the great potential of mankind and a personal future beyond this world. They go forth, multiply, and strive for a better world for themselves and their children. But these true believers make up a small minority. Unfortunately our religious organizations do not have the knowledge and are too weak to stand up to the intimidating power of scientific knowledge.

Most of the world's population is drifting away from God, providence, and heaven, resulting in the human race's slide into a world full of people that only believe in themselves and what they can get out of their time on Earth. Whole societies no longer care about the future. They are not even having enough children to replace themselves, and so their cultures soon will cease to exist. If this drift away from the Supreme Being does not reverse, then humanity is doomed.

We look into the night sky and wonder what it's all about. Should we care about how the universe works or just live life as it comes? We all know we are participating in a physical reality, but we don't stop to think very much about it or how we fit into the physical action taking place all around us. Each of us goes about a daily routine of working, taking care of family, and trying to make the most out of the circumstances into which we were born. We might even attend church hoping that we will go to heaven, although we're not sure. Mathematics, biology, chemistry, and theoretical physics all seem too complicated, so we give the job of defining our world to our expert scientists. But should we? Although we share this reality, we each experience it alone on a solo journey. It is certain that someday each one of us will die and leave this world. Maybe it would be better if we had some understanding about our human role in the process.

Mortality is the single most important question each of us will confront during our brief life on Earth. Is this all there is, or will we live on in another life? Are we insignificant beings lost in space and time, or are we special beings created by God? An individual's mortality is such a difficult issue that most people avoid even discussing it. Then one day he or she suddenly faces the unknown alone.

Melville's nineteenth-century novel *Moby Dick* is a metaphor for the human struggle to come to terms with reality. At first it is a story about a sea captain obsessed to right the wrong against him by getting revenge on a whale for biting off his leg; however, the story has much deeper meaning. The great white whale represents God, creation, and reality. Captain Ahab represents our human confrontation with the universe. Ahab becomes consumed with the struggle, and his inability to understand causes him to become bitter and hateful. His battle with Moby Dick ends with his own destruction. Melville's message is that the universe is so impossibly complex that you will waste your life trying to figure it out.

We must ignore Melville, because it is modern science that makes life seem impossibly complex and meaningless. You will waste your life if you don't understand your journey. Melville wrongly thought that humans are inherently incapable of understanding the universe. If you take his advice, you will abdicate your natural power and influence. Even if your religious faith is strong, you still need to understand how the process physically works to truly understand your place in the cosmos.

We have all struggled to understand. When we were young, our growing minds soaked up knowledge like a sponge. We learned by observing and listening to people around us. Our parents told us what they believed. Many of our families practiced a particular religion, and we were taught a particular version of creation. Then we went to school, and our teachers taught us the scientific definition of everything. We had to sort through a lot of conflicting information.

Life today is confusing. Science is strong, but disconnected and confusing. And religion has lost its way. People are overwhelmed, but even so it is falsely believed that today's science is on the right track. Even the world's religions are attempting to adjust their doctrines to fit today's scientific views. The Roman Catholic Church has finally given in; the pope officially pardoned Galileo for starting the modern scientific revolution and removing humans from the center of everything. Modern people have been forced to come to terms with the thought that they are very small fish in a very big pond and what they think or do has no effect beyond their own personal experience here on Earth.

But despite the confusion and complexity of the current scientific view, we should not be overpowered by the world around us. This book will show that the cosmos is only as big and complex as the prevailing human technical capability. There is nothing that does exist that can be shown to be beyond human comprehension. This book will solve the mystery of matter and show that we humans do have the capacity to understand the universe and how we fit into it. This book will show that our material universe does not stand alone. This book will prove that a higher being (God) is responsible for creating and looking over the continued existence of humanity and all we see around us.

CHAPTER TWO

What Does Matter Have to Do With It?

How does our material universe exist? Did it spontaneously arise from nothing without help as scientists claim, or did a higher being create it? In order to find out how a material thing exists, you must investigate the parts that make up the thing. If you can determine how the parts are made and what they are made of, then you can understand how the thing came to exist in the first place. This is true for all things big and small.

Our universe is the biggest thing we know of, but it still must be investigated the same way. Our entire material universe is made of something scientists call matter. So, if you know what fundamental matter is and how it exists in the first place, then you know how our whole universe came to exist in the first place. If you find out that matter is freestanding (exists without help), then God is not necessary for our universe to exist. If you find out, however, that matter cannot exist without outside help, then there is no other answer except there is something beyond our physical world (a higher power) that caused and is causing it to exist.

When you first examine some physical object or system of objects, you have no way of knowing how it works or much else about it, because you had no part in designing it or installing it in the first place. You can take it for granted, but then you will never understand how or why it does what it does. I have learned to understand how systems work through reverse engineering. You can examine the parts of the system to see how they fit together and determine how they were made, what they are made of, and how all of the pieces are controlled together to function as a working, continuous process. Only then can you understand the whole design and figure out the designer's intent. This book is about reverse engineering the universe.

Maybe it will always be impossible for us earthlings to know the actual realm of God and souls until we go there, because we do not have the intellect to understand how nonphysical things like souls and thoughts can exist in the first place. This book will show that we do have the intellect to know how our material world came to exist in the beginning. We can scientifically trace the evidence from the inside out and solve the mysteries of the universe. We can understand the universe, how we fit into it, and whether or not a greater being is responsible through knowing the nature of its design and what it is made of. The ultimate target of the investigation is the mystery of matter.

Scientists know that every single thing in our universe is made of something they call matter—even our human bodies. Our material world is one big system that functions as a continuous process, and everything is made of different combinations of the same basic particles. Scientists can look at anything through a microscope and see smaller and smaller particles, which all ultimately are made of matter. Scientists can measure these particles and their movements, but even after hundreds of years of scientific effort, they cannot figure out what matter actually is or how it got here. They just keep finding smaller forms of matter (particles).

Modern science misses the point and focuses on the particles and not the ultimate question of matter. A particle is a form of matter. A form of matter does not tell us what matter is. We need to know what matter actually is, not what types of particles it is made into. If we can understand what matter actually is and how it exists in the first place, then we can figure out what our whole physical universe actually is, how it exists in the first place, and whether or not God created it. Unfortunately, scientists just skip over the modern scientific model's inability to understand matter. Scientists say that matter simply exists, but this is not science.

Matter should be the most important scientific question to everyone in our modern world, because understanding matter is the key to understanding the human journey through space and time. Therefore I need to begin by establishing the concept of matter in the reader's mind. I have found that this is a difficult concept for most people, so let's start with a hypothetical situation to illustrate what I mean.

Imagine a realm where many nonphysical beings exist. These beings do not have physical bodies, and there is no material world in which to live. But the nonphysical beings do have self-awareness and they do have thoughts, both of which are nonphysical. In this realm there is a supreme being who wants all beings to have the best possible existence, so all are free to have their own thoughts. And all is good and wonderful in the realm.

Then, some of the beings begin to take advantage of their freedom. They start having bad thoughts, and this becomes more and more of a problem. The once joyous and righteous realm starts to deteriorate. The supreme being realizes that bad could become evil, so some changes must be made. The supreme being knows that free will is most important in his realm, so it is most important *not* to control how the beings think. The supreme being decides to let the problem beings directly experience the difference between good and evil, so they might find out for themselves what the best thoughts are. He decides that all the problem beings should physically act out their thoughts in a physical universe. Then, after seeing the error of their ways, they can return to the realm where every being is again free and filled with righteousness.

The supreme being asks for ideas for a design of a physical universe that will fit his concept. There are many proposals, but he only considers two possibilities. The first proposal the supreme being considers is to create a freestanding physical reality that will be completely separate from his greater, nonphysical realm. The plan is to create physical bodies for the beings as an integral part of a common universe design, so all living life forms can interact and evolve within the same physical process. The supreme being will then set the whole system in motion under its own power. The problem beings will be on their own to learn their lessons without help from him. Once all of the problem beings learn that good triumphs over evil, he will remove the physical reality and bring them all back to his realm.

In order for the free beings to continuously interact in a physical world, the design specifies a three-dimensional reality with forward-moving time. It will be necessary to build the freestanding world out of something that can exist by itself without help from the nonphysical realm—some kind of fundamental, self-contained physical object. Everything will be made of this smallest building block particle. This fundamental particle cannot contain anything itself (or it would not be fundamental), and it will be indivisible (indestructible).

However, after the supreme being gives more thought to this design, he realizes it has many flaws and will not work the way he wants it to. The point of the physical universe is to give the beings an opportunity to reform themselves due to their free will actions. In order for this to happen, the beings must be able to personally influence their surroundings by being directly connected to their material world. They must have the capability of acting out their free will, so their physical surroundings must be designed to be directly influenced by their thoughts. If the physical universe is designed to exist and evolve on its own without a direct connection to the beings, then they will not be able to interact freely. They will be limited to the capabilities of their physical bodies and be pulled along by the cause and effect of the unfolding universe processes. The beings will be unable to exercise their free will and therefore unable to redeem themselves. Nothing they do will be either an achievement or a fault of their own.

And the more the supreme being considers it, the more he realizes that even he does not know how to create an indivisible, freestanding particle disconnected from his nonphysical realm. What will it be made of? There isn't anything to make it out of. There is no such thing as a purely physical substance. The only way he knows how to create and sustain a physical object is through pure thought. If he quits thinking about it and leaves it on its own, then it will no longer exist. He realizes that he can't create a disconnected physical universe even if he wants to.

Also, the supreme being wants the beings to be tied to their own actions and not to the decisions of the other beings. He wants to give each being the capability of individual redemption. He doesn't like the plan to wait for all of the problem beings to understand the difference between good and evil and then for all to choose good before bringing all of them back. He realizes that freedom means that some may never choose good over evil.

The supreme being begins to study the second proposal, and he immediately likes what he sees because it is not a freestanding reality. It will be continuously connected to his nonphysical realm. In fact the physical object world will be a materialization of the free beings' thoughts. Even though each being will be residing in a physical body, each will still be a free soul, able to push, pull, and mold its own material world while still connected to the supreme being. The souls will be free to act as they please and can individually come back if and when they redeem themselves.

This second proposal had some design features of the first proposal, because it also needs three dimensions of space and forward-moving time. And the inhabitants' bodies are an integral part of this universe's design, so everything can evolve and interact seamlessly. It is not, however, a limited, freestanding universe as in the first proposal; instead it has no boundaries, big or small. If something is freestanding, then it must have edges or boundaries, or it could not exist by itself. By the nature of its design, this second proposal will be limited only by the beings' imaginations, which are unlimited.

The supreme being immediately knows how to create and sustain a physical world made from the nonphysical world. He knows that he and the other free souls of his realm can create volumetric space through their own thought processes. So he designs the physical reality to be based on a mathematical program (nonphysical) that can convert thought-generated space into physical particles.

The supreme being creates a sink (miniature black hole) and lets the surrounding space flow downward into it. As space flows down, the space becomes more and more compressed into a smaller and smaller volume, which causes the space to accelerate (imagine water going down a funnel). The flow is not continuously smooth; at specific rates of acceleration and at specific places, the fluid space rotates and vibrates around the sink. These highly accelerated parts of space become what the beings will detect as solid particles.

This is just the design the supreme being is looking for. He also knows that forces are required to make the whole reality function as a continuously connected system, and this matter creation process, he realizes, will do the trick.

Space and time come from the nonphysical realm (pure thought). The supreme being designed a physical reality made out of space-time. When space is accelerated it becomes physical matter (mass). Mass $(m) = d^3/t^2$.

These are the mathematical relationships the supreme being used in defining this physical particle: a volume of space has three dimensions—distance (d) x distance (d) x distance (d) = d^3; flowing space with constant velocity $(Q) = d^3/t$; and space accelerating = flowing space with changing velocity = mass = $dQ/dt = d^3/t^2$. (This mathematical definition of matter will become clearer and more connected when the unified equation of the universe is presented in a later chapter.)

Through his thought process, the supreme being used accelerated space to generate all physical objects and all the forces of nature required for his beings to physically interact with each other. Each free being would interact within the rules of the program. The program would allow the solid manifestation of their world to materialize on each free being's viewing screen. Their direct connection to their environment would allow each being to push and pull their surroundings for better or worse. And since they were also directly connected to the greater realm, they could individually return if and when they redeemed themselves.

This book will prove that our real physical universe is in fact made up of a matter creation process just like in the preceding hypothetical reality.

Now we need to change to our own real, modern times. We humans are imbedded in our reality, so we can only analyze the universe from inside of it. Isaac Newton, arguably the greatest scientist in history, believed in God because he thought a physical thing had to be created in the first place. He did not think God was active in our lives, however; he thought things simply existed. He thought the universe was created and set in motion to operate under its own power.

Today's scientists have gone even further to remove God from our lives. They have examined the universe, determined that everything can be explained by science, and found no evidence of a supreme being. They claim God does not exist or, in any case, is unnecessary. At best they see the universe as being similar to the supreme being's first proposal. Scientists overlook the fact that they really can't explain what matter is and cannot prove we live in a freestanding universe.

The rest of this book should convince you that our universe is not freestanding without God. This book will prove that God exists by proving that the universe does not exist out there by itself; the universe in which each of us lives comes from the nonphysical realm of God and souls.

The scientific evidence presented in this book proves that our universe is like the supreme being's second proposal: created and watched over by God.

CHAPTER THREE

The Confused State of Science

Scientists would have us believe that we are nothing more than sophisticated animals. Animals live as if they are simply here. Most modern human beings do too, but they should not, because humans are capable of much more.

I have always wanted to really understand how it is that I exist. Don't you? Every day of my life I have thought in amazement about the fact that I am actually here, experiencing this world. I don't know how a person can really look at life and believe it is all an accident of nature. If it is, then where did nature come from?

It is logical to define reality as consisting of two possible states: physical or nonphysical. And since something cannot just magically exist, it is logical that the physical must come from the nonphysical. The nonphysical must be the first state. So, it would seem that our physical reality comes from a greater nonphysical realm. Therefore, it makes logical sense that there is more beyond what we humans can sense or otherwise measure, but how can it be scientifically proven if scientists cannot sense and measure it?

When I was five years old I believed in God because I was taught that this is how the world works. I thought at this young age that if life on Earth is hard and short and life in heaven is good and forever, then going to heaven should be the main goal for everybody, because what happens on Earth is temporary. I asked my mom, "Do all preachers go to heaven?" I wondered why everyone wasn't a preacher. I found out later that being a preacher is not necessarily a ticket to heaven.

During my childhood, some of my friends said they did not believe in God, because there was no evidence that He existed. They said evolution explained it all. I thought about evolution and concluded it could explain how existing life changes over time, but I couldn't understand how the universe—no matter how small—could materialize from nothing to something. I thought it had to take more than evolution to accomplish that.

My Sunday school teacher and my preacher said I must have blind faith in God and creation, but blind faith was not enough for me. And I thought that the biblical stories were not very believable—I wanted hard evidence. If there was no God, then I wanted to know that. If there was a God, then I wanted to know that for sure. I wanted the truth, wherever that might lead.

After thinking about it for a few years (during which time I learned about scientific universe theories), I asked my dad how he thought everything worked. He wasn't sure. I said I didn't think that the pieces of the puzzle fit with either the religious version or the scientific version of reality. I speculated that things must work in an entirely different way. He thought I was probably right. I set out on a long quest to learn everything I could about the universe. I wanted to learn everything scientists knew and more. I wanted all of the pieces of the puzzle to fit together.

During my childhood I would spend long hours alone, thinking. At times I would drift into what appeared to be a physical reality within myself. These inward journeys were not the same as my night dreams. This controlled inner reality was as real and vivid as my outer world. I could not tell the difference. From these personal experiences, I learned that a mind-generated reality works the same way a real outer reality works. Obviously my inner reality was not made of solid, freestanding objects, but I could not tell that it was not. It became clear that my real outer reality was not necessarily solid, freestanding, or disconnected from me either.

Although I intuitively thought this was a clue to understanding the universe, scientists dismissed this kind of experience altogether, because it could not be explored or measured. At this time in my life I was not capable of understanding how this could be explained in scientific terms, so I continued to study all I could about science. I knew that I had to acquire much more knowledge about how the scientific universe model worked before I could understand what was wrong with it.

I did not necessarily attend college to prepare for a career. My main purpose was to gain as much technical knowledge as possible in order to understand the universe. As a beginning student, I thought that mathematics was just a convenient human invention that made it possible for people to manage their daily lives, such as performing financial transactions, keeping track of inventories, designing buildings, and constructing public works. I thought the universe might be far too complex and disconnected to figure out.

I was as yet unaware that mathematics is fundamental to the construction and operation of the entire physical universe. Then I studied Isaac Newton's laws of motion and universal law of gravitation, which show that everything in the cosmos is universally tied together by simple mathematical rules. For example, the act of a child throwing a ball follows the same mathematical rule as a comet orbiting the sun. For me this knowledge brought a comforting unification to my universe. It became clear that the cosmos is not really chaotic or disconnected. It behaves as one large, interconnected, ordered process. Because the universe can be understood mathematically, I realized that scientists have the power to understand how the entire universe works. I wondered why the fundamental mysteries were still unsolved.

Mathematics is a universal language that describes the ratios or relationships between the things in our reality. It cannot be scientifically shown that any object large or small has independent size. Size means nothing except when comparing one thing to another.

For example, we describe the size of the earth by comparing it to the size of the human body. There is no other way to do it. We assign sizes to everything in the known universe as fractions or multiples of our own size. A foot distance is an arbitrary standard unit that originated by marking off the length of a man's foot. A mile is a standard unit that is 5,280 feet—or 5,280 times the length of a past man's foot (probably a king's foot). So when we say the earth is eight thousand miles in diameter, we are not saying it takes up a specific amount of free space; we are saying that the earth's diameter is 42,240,000 times the length of a man's foot. Everything is relative to everything else, and mathematics gives us a universal way to describe how things fit together.

By investigating and measuring how things work, we can figure out mathematical relationships. Then mathematical equations can be developed that model the process and tell us how it will act in the future. All physical processes consist of interacting objects, so all processes can be described using mathematical models. The whole universe is no different, even though it is the biggest of all processes; however, all parts of the process must be understood, or as in today's disconnected scientific world-view, the formulations will be disconnected and the mathematical model will not truly be representative.

The modern nonhuman scientific model was developed over several centuries. It replaced an ancient, human-centered model. The foundation of the modern model is not based on scientific facts, though; it is based on human perceptions.

Pre-modern scientists believed in God, so science used to be concerned with explaining God's creation. The pre-modern model worked well for thousands of years. It had a fixed Earth with the sun, moon, planets, and stars revolving around it. We now know that this model was technically wrong, but these people did not yet have the technical capability to explore and more thoroughly understand the solar system.

In this human-centered world-view, people intuitively knew they were at the center of everything that exists. People believed they were special beings created by God. Then a so-called renaissance took place in Western Europe. Science started taking an independent path from religion, and a new, non-human-centered model began to replace the old, human-centered model.

Nicolaus Copernicus was a Polish astronomer who confronted the church's earth-centered universe. Copernicus's book *On the Revolutions of the Celestial Spheres* was published just before his death in 1543. The thesis of Copernicus's theory is that the earth rotates daily on its axis and revolves yearly around the sun. It also states that the planets also circle the sun, and that the earth precesses on its axis (wobbles like a top) as it rotates.

Copernicus's theory kept many features of the system it replaced, including the planet-bearing spheres and the outermost sphere bearing the fixed stars. But Copernicus's heliocentric theory of planetary motion accounted for the daily and yearly motion of the sun and stars. It also precisely explained the retrograde motion of Mars, Jupiter, and Saturn and accounted for the fact that Mercury and Venus never move more than a short distance from the sun.

Copernicus didn't publish his work until just before his death, because he feared criticism from the scientists and theologians. His theories supposedly denied the earth was at the center of the universe, something the church had been teaching for over a thousand years. To many it even seemed to contradict the Bible. In the century after its publication, the church officially condemned Copernicus's theory.

However, after at first being rejected, by the late seventeenth century the Copernican universe model was the most accepted concept of the universe, because it was simpler and matched well with increasingly more precise observations and measurements.

People gradually became aware that if Copernicus's theory was right, then the most trusted of all authorities had to be wrong, including the Bible, the church, and the wisest men in the history of the world. And if they were wrong about how the solar system works, then they must be wrong about other things too. It no longer seemed that everything revolved around humanity. Once the greater population came to this realization, it was a world-changing consequence for human attitudes, mainly toward religion. The entire established order of things was questioned.

The fifteenth and sixteenth centuries were a period of sweeping social, political, and intellectual change. Changes included the Reformation, the exploration of the world, and the rise of commercialism. New ideas appeared in all areas of culture. The medieval world as a hierarchy created and governed by God was replaced by a mechanical view of the world operating as a vast machine, moving according to physical laws with no purpose or will.

The goal of life in this world was no longer envisioned as preparation for salvation in life after death. People now wanted to live out their natural desires.

Government institutions and moral principles were no longer attributed to divine power. These things were now considered to be creations of humanity. Experience and reason became the principle standards of truth in this new secular world-view.

Galileo Galilei was born in Italy in 1564. He became a professor of mathematics at the University of Pisa, Italy, where he confirmed the error of Aristotle, who was up until this time the unquestioned authority on almost all things. Galileo rolled balls of unequal weights down an inclined plane and proved that the speed of fall is not proportional to weight. His discoveries included the laws of falling bodies and the parabolic paths of projectiles. Galileo also studied the motions of pendulums and investigated mechanics and the strength of materials.

In early 1609 Galileo found out that a spyglass had been invented in Holland. He immediately constructed a telescope of twenty times magnification with which he observed mountains and craters on the moon. He also saw that the Milky Way was composed of stars, and he discovered the four largest moons of Jupiter. He published his findings in 1610 in the *Starry Messenger*. Also in this same year he confirmed the Copernican model by observing the phases of Venus.

Galileo was much more critical than Copernicus. Galileo actually questioned the very foundation of Christian doctrine. He was held in contempt for his discoveries because belief in a moving Earth was considered heretical. In 1616 Cardinal Robert Bellarmine instructed Galileo that he must no longer support or even believe in the concept of a moving Earth. After a long silence, Galileo wrote about Copernican theory again in relation to the physics of the tides in a book published in 1632. In 1633 he was summoned to Rome by the Inquisition to stand trial on suspicion of heresy. The result was that he was sentenced to life imprisonment, although his imprisonment was commuted to permanent house arrest. Galileo died in 1642, not long before Isaac Newton was born.

Galileo was at the center of the development of the new, scientific world-view. His main involvement was the founding of physics on precise measurements, which replaced Aristotle's metaphysical principles and formal logic. Galileo stressed the importance of applying mathematics to the formulation of scientific laws. He created the science of mechanics, which applied the principles of geometry to the motion of bodies.

The success of mechanics in discovering the laws of nature persuaded Galileo and future scientists that all of nature operates strictly in accordance with mechanical laws. Galileo's invention of the scientific method started the modern scientific revolution, which led to the discovery of a vast and previously unknown universe. This change in perspective changed people's ideas of life in the universe and their relationships to God. They now began to believe they were purposeless beings stranded on a remote and insignificant planet somewhere within an overpowering universe.

Sir Isaac Newton, the greatest scientist in history, was born in 1642 in Lincolnshire, England. In 1666, at age 24, he generalized the methods used to draw tangents to curves and to calculate the area swept by curves. He understood that these two methods were inverse procedures, so he joined them in a completely new mathematics he called the "fluxional method," which is now known as calculus.

During this same time period Gottfried Wilhelm Leibniz independently discovered nearly the same method, which he called "differential calculus." Leibniz published before Newton, but Newton did his work earlier.

Calculus was a breakthrough discovery that carried mathematics above the level of Greek geometry. Calculus made it possible to mathematically determine the instantaneous interactions between objects in space and time. Using calculus, scientists could much more accurately measure how the universe acts.

In the 1680s Newton found inspiration in a discussion with British astronomer and mathematician Edmund Halley (discoverer of Halley's Comet) about orbital motion. This inspiration led to Newton's formulating his three laws of motion, which in turn led to the modern science of dynamics. When Newton applied these laws to German astronomer Johannes Kepler's laws of orbital motion, he derived the law of universal gravitation.

Newton's law of universal gravitation explains how all objects are acted upon by the force of gravity. He detailed these findings in his famous book *Philosophae Naturalis Principia Mathematica*, which was a breakthrough in science and changed the universe model forever. (Newton's formula defined the effect gravity has on objects, but neither he nor any other scientist has ever understood what gravity is or where it comes from.)

Only fifty-four years earlier, Galileo had been condemned for claiming the earth moves around the sun. Now Newton mapped out an accurate working model of the entire planetary system. Newton's work established what appeared to be a complete picture of reality. His equations for motion and gravity seemingly gave scientists the means to explain everything. Based on his work, it was believed that the workings of the universe were subject to laws; that these laws were discernible by human beings; and that they were expressible in mathematical equations.

These equations gave scientists the power to understand and predict nature. Scientists theorized that when given a particular present state, its future state could be calculated. Everything could be determined as it moved in absolute space in absolute time. This gave scientists a sense of power over nature. Newtonian mechanics became instrumental in the development of the machinery that made the coming industrial revolution a reality. This amazing success made scientists feel as if they were becoming the masters of the universe.

However, the earth was no longer believed to be the center of that universe. It was now seen as a minor planet revolving around a minor star, so it became difficult for most to believe that the existence of the entire cosmos had a purpose connected with humanity. How could anyone believe that humans had free will when scientific laws determined the actions of everything, including humans, and therefore everything was predetermined? A widespread disbelief in the existence of God, which has continued to this day, began to characterize western civilization. But even with this outlook, Newton still believed in some sort of an initial Creator, because he thought something must have been responsible for starting everything in the first place.

Newton's world-view was widely accepted for approximately two hundred years, during which time his laws were applied to the movements of all objects in the known human reality. Newtonian scientists believed that gravity was the only force in the universe, and they thought they completely understood how the whole universe worked.

Newton's world-view is now known as classical physics, because it was the first, although it has been superseded by relativity and quantum mechanics.

Until 1887 no flaw was found in Newton's physics. But that year the Michelson–Morley experiment (named after the American physicist Albert Michelson and the American chemist Edward Morley) was performed. Up until this time, it was assumed that a hypothetical, mass-less substance called "aether" permeated space. The aether was thought to be necessary to transmit electromagnetic radiation, including visible light. Michelson deduced that the earth must move relative to the aether. The experiment was an attempt to determine the earth's rate of motion through the aether.

As the sun and the entire solar system move through space, the constantly changing direction of the earth's orbit causes the velocity of the earth relative to the sun to be added to or subtracted from the velocity of the sun at different times of the year. The result of the experiment was entirely unexpected. The velocity of the earth through the hypothetical aether was found to be zero at all times of the year. Science was again in a quandary. Scientists wondered what space was made of.

As science and scientific instruments became more sophisticated, a variety of very small objects were found at the so-called foundation of our reality. Newton's equations could not explain or predict the motions of these atomic world objects, so scientists had to go back to work to find new theories and new equations to explain the changing model of nature. Electric and magnetic forces were discovered to be responsible for making the small part of reality work. Further research found that electricity and magnetism are aspects of the same force, and electromagnetism was added with gravity as a duo that accounts for all movement.

Since the time of Newton, scientists have been trying to understand the nature of matter and radiation and how they interact in some unified world picture. The position that mechanical laws are fundamental has become known as the mechanical world-view, and the position that electrical laws are fundamental has become known as the electromagnetic world-view. Neither approach is capable of providing a consistent explanation for the interaction between radiation (light, for example) and matter when viewed from different frames of reference.

Albert Einstein was a German-born theoretical physicist. He was born in 1879 just at the right time to tackle the aether mystery. He is considered the most influential scientist of the twentieth-century. Einstein became world famous for his development of the theory of relativity and the discovery that matter and energy are equivalent. This equivalency relationship is expressed in the equation $E = mc^2$.

As a boy and a young man Einstein contemplated the problems of the missing aether and the transmission of light through space. While working as a clerk in a Swiss patent office Einstein was fortunate to be assigned the job of evaluating patent applications pertaining to the transmission of electric signals. He found that Newtonian physics could not explain light propagation or the problems associated with the synchronization of time.

In 1905 Einstein published a paper that later became known as the special theory of relativity. He did not address the question of what things are made of or what matter ultimately is. He addressed the problem not as a theory of matter but as a theory of measurement. The theory of relativity was able to consistently describe physical actions in different inertial frames of reference without involving the question of the aether or the nature matter. After the introduction of relativity, scientists assumed the aether was unnecessary to explain the universe and claimed it did not even exist.

Einstein wrote four scientific papers in his famous year of 1905. One of them was the discovery of the photoelectric effect. It was a revolutionary discovery about the nature of light. In the past, Newton and all other scientists up until1905 believed light was propagated in a continuous stream, but Einstein proposed that light is transmitted in individual units, or quanta. Einstein played a big part in the development of quantum theory, but he did not accept the theoretical uncertainty of the quantum world. He could not believe that God plays dice.

Ten years later in 1915, Einstein tackled the question of the source of gravity in his general theory of relativity. Again, he did not see it as a question of what space actually is or the nature of matter. He theorized that space-time, whatever it is or wherever it comes from, bends in the presence of massive objects like our Sun. This phenomenon, he claimed, was what caused gravitational attraction. An often used analogy would be a golf ball curving on a warped putting green. Einstein assumed that the physical universe simply does exist needing no further scientific explanation. He was following in the footsteps of Aristotle, Galileo and Newton by believing the universe exists as a freestanding assembly of things.

During the remainder of his life, Einstein tried in vain to come up with a scientific explanation that would connect all of nature and nature's forces into a single theory of everything. He died in 1955, and since then no other scientist has fared any better.

From 1915 to 1930 science was concerned with developing a theory describing and predicting the fundamental particles at what was thought to be at the very foundation of the universe. Quantum theory defines the universe as consisting of discrete particles or packets of electrical energy called quanta and is used to describe and predict the smaller part of the universe that we cannot directly experience. Scientists are baffled that sometimes the universe is measured as being made of waves, while at other times it is measured as being made of particles.

Scientists also found that precision in measuring the quantum world is uncertain. Calculations and predictions of events in terms of statistical probability have replaced the deterministic cause-and-effect relationships inherent in Newtonian mechanics. Quantum mechanics has helped scientists predict the particle movements within the most complex atoms. Today our modern scientific model of reality is based on the disconnected theories of relativity and quantum mechanics. Newton's classical physics is considered a special case of Einstein's relativity. Relativity defines the relationships between objects in four-dimensional space-time and is used to describe and predict the actions of the larger world we humans actually experience.

Newtonian mechanics is still the most practical tool for scientists to measure and predict the actions of our everyday human world, but today's focus of science is on understanding the fundamental particles in nature. Therefore quantum mechanics is the mathematical tool that scientists use most.

Theoretical physicists have taken over where Einstein left off. Over the last few decades, there have been many strange and complicated efforts to explain how everything works, but all of these efforts have failed to unite all of the known forces of nature or to explain how our universe exists. Particle physicists continue to search for a theory of everything (TOE), and the most recent best hope has been the theory of superstrings. This is an enormously complicated attempt suggesting that everything in the universe—including all particles, forces, and space-time—consist of infinitesimally small strings under immense tension, vibrating and spinning in ten-dimensional super space. After initial hopefulness, superstring theory has not lived up to expectations and has fallen on hard times.

Scientists claim their best answer to where everything came from is the big bang theory. They have measured the motions of the galaxies in outer space and concluded they are all moving away from each other at a highly accelerated rate of speed. In other words the whole universe is expanding. This action is plotted backward, and it is calculated that the whole universe began approximately fifteen billion years ago as a small, very dense, atom-sized glob of matter/energy. Theoretically all the things we see and experience today are evolutionary results of this original miniature universe that exploded. But how did this first primal version of the universe get here?

Scientists are trying to explain how the universe began by describing what it might have physically looked like in the past, but a beginning freestanding universe would have to contain something too. This starting universe would not have been insignificant. It would have to have been extremely complex and only considered small when compared to today's universe. In fact there would have to have been all the ingredients that led to today's very complex reality. The big bang theory describes modern scientists' version of how our universe has acted, but it does not explain what our universe is made up of or how it exists in the first place.

Defining the universe as an expanding freestanding assembly of objects indicates that the universe is expanding into something else that already exists. If space is a volumetric void, then what is it a void in? Science's best answer to this question is that our four-dimensional reality is expanding into a fifth dimension, but how would a fifth dimension get here? It is not enough to just say that dimensions are magically here. If the universe exists as a freestanding thing, then where does it exist? Who can explain where the initial "here" is? If there is a here, then there is more.

The problem with these and all other scientific mysteries is that our reality (space, time, and matter) is not what scientists think it is. It is not a freestanding, physical thing. Physical things cannot just simply be here.

If the universe began with a "big bang" explosion, then today's physical world would consist of objects flying through space with trajectories originating from a single speck of plasma. There would be no direct connection between humanity and the vast universe in the earth's night sky. And we humans would be, as science claims, accidental by-products of nature. Belief in this theory would cause a person to think of the universe as being much too complex and removed from humanity for our lowly human brain to ever understand. But if everything were really so disconnected and beyond our intellect, then how is it that the universe is governed by mathematical rules that we are able to understand?

Particle scientists are working on what they call their standard model theory, which they hope will eventually explain all particles and forces in one unified, freestanding theory of everything. Scientists are trying to put twelve so-called fundamental building blocks particles (known and unknown) into an arrangement that defines an absolute foundation to the universe. A very large effort is focused on finding the missing theoretical Higgs Boson particle, which scientists claim is the source of mass and gravitational force for the entire universe. The other particles supposedly get their mass from the Higgs particle. The activity is concentrated at the European Organization for Nuclear Research (CERN). Physicists are using the Large Hadron Collider (LHC) to hunt down this very mysterious and supposedly all-important particle. Once again scientists believe they are on the right path to completely defining a freestanding universe.

This kind of thinking reminds me of Ptolemy, the ancient Greek scientist and mathematician. He scientifically defined a freestanding, earth-centered solar system, but his theory had to become more and more complicated as time went on in order to make it match man's constantly increasing knowledge of the physical world. It eventually failed to live up to expectations and was discarded as a viable model of the universe. Things have not changed.

The scientists at CERN probably will confirm that the Higgs Boson particle exists. I have learned in my career that researchers with preconceived goals usually manage to find what they are looking and measuring for, because their research is biased in favor of a desired outcome. Lifetime careers depend on it. They ignore or minimize any unfavorable information. It will make no difference in the long run. This theory is doomed to ultimately fail, as have all other attempts to define a freestanding universe, because scientists are describing how the universe acts but not what it ultimately *is*.

A Higgs Boson particle, like all particles, is a form of matter, and a form of matter does not give any clue as to what matter actually is or how it exists in the first place. What is a Higgs Boson particle made of? The particle physicists at CERN would say it is indivisible and therefore made of nothing. Apparently it takes people outside of mainstream science to realize that this answer smacks of magic and not science. The Higgs Boson particle, if it exists, is made of matter, and freestanding-trained scientists will never have a clue.

Scientists such as Copernicus, Galileo, Newton, and Einstein were very successful in figuring out how the objects in our reality interact, so they are responsible for humans having some control over nature and for many developments in the modern world. Unfortunately, their tremendous success has given people the false impression that science knows enough about the universe to also determine that God is not responsible for it. The truth is that these scientists—as well as all others—have failed to prove how anything came to exist in the first place, let alone whether or not God exists.

There is nothing wrong with modern scientific discovery. Classical physics, relativity, and quantum mechanics work very well. These theories are tried and tested on the real world. The problem is with interpreting the larger world-view. Western science, starting with Aristotle and the ancient Greeks, has assumed that the universe is freestanding, and ever since Copernicus's heliocentric theory and Galileo's discoveries, science has misinterpreted the earth's moving around the sun to mean that humans are not really at the center of everything. The modern world-view is not based on scientific fact; it is based on false assumptions and interpretations.

It all comes down to a question of what matter is and how matter exists. Scientists cannot figure out the universe because it does not work the way they think it does. They are looking for something that does not exist. There are no smallest freestanding particles of which everything is made. The universe works in a completely different way from the way scientists think it does. Science has travelled down a long, dead-end road.

CHAPTER FOUR

The Search for Understanding

I learned from my experience as a research engineer that in order to solve difficult problems, you first must thoroughly study and investigate the system in question. You must acquire intimate knowledge of the system and how it works, which means both theory and real world experience.

The universe is no different. What is a force of nature? What is gravity? What is electricity? How are the fundamental forces connected together? Scientists know how parts of the universe work separately, but they have no idea how it all ties together as a complete, connected system. These mysteries are all connected. As the Greek philosopher Thales understood two and a half millennia ago, when we know what matter is and how it exists, then we will understand the underlying design of the whole universe and how it works as a connected process.

Newton's universe was believed to be infinitely large—but how can a freestanding material universe be infinite? That means it continues forever and is filled with an infinite number of objects. A scientist would not be able to objectively define such a reality. How big is it? What is in it? Infinity seems to be a human perception and not a real possibility.

Einstein tried to get around the infinity problem by claiming the universe curves back on itself. But, I wonder, how can a volume of space—even if it does curve back on itself—exist in nothing? There would be a boundary problem. It seems to me that Einstein came up with a convoluted universe in an attempt to retain a freestanding universe model, but he failed, as have all other attempts at explaining a freestanding universe.

The big bang theory also would need to pass the infinity and boundary problems, which it does not.

Today's particle physicists are having infinity and boundary problems at the inner edge, or so-called foundation of our reality.

As a child, like many curious children, I took mechanisms apart to see what they were made of and how they work. I studied how the parts inside of machines interact. One of my first explorations was taking apart old clocks. Clocks are ingenious devices with many parts, which must work together flawlessly. The parts must be very precise and interact with extremely low friction, so the clock can operate with low power and last a long time before wearing out.

The first accurate clocks were pendulum clocks. The steady pull of gravity causes a swinging pendulum to always sweep back and forth at the same time interval, no matter the distance of the swing. The length of the pendulum can be adjusted so that the time of the sweep exactly coincides with a desired time interval. In this way the clock can be made to repeatedly tic off seconds, minutes, and hours. Hanging weights and gravity provide the force that keeps the pendulum swinging.

Pendulum clocks do not work at sea, because the pitching and rolling of the ship prevent a smooth and steady operation. Spring power was the answer to keeping accurate time at sea, but it took a long time before spring-powered mechanisms could be perfected to the point where the diminishing force of an unwinding spring could be regulated to maintain a constant movement over many days, weeks, and months.

Clock makers became the first highly skilled machinists. Many other industries such as gun manufacturing later relied on these clock-makers' skills to produce the accurate parts required to make their products work properly.

Clockwork has become a metaphor for all fine-working machinery.

Learning about the operation of mechanisms such as clocks did not satisfy my curiosity about the mechanical universe. I wanted to know what the parts of things are made of, and I wanted to know what the parts of the parts of the parts are made of. It seemed to me that everything has to be made of something, but where does the downward discovery stop? Where is the starting point to the universe? Is there a limit to how small something can be? If the physical universe exists as a freestanding assembly of parts, then there has to be a fundamental part of which everything is made, and this smallest of all objects cannot be made of anything itself. I wondered how this could be possible. I wanted to know how the universe could exist by itself, and where did the original part come from? As I later found out, this is the dilemma of today's science.

When we explore matter through a microscope, we see an amazing assembly of things. When we look deep inside an object, we find that it is constructed of smaller objects called molecules. When we look inside the molecules, we find that they are constructed of even smaller objects called atoms. Scientists have broken atoms apart and found smaller objects inside them. The interior of these sub-atomic particles have also been investigated, and much smaller things have been found there. This is the limit of today's detection and measurement technology, but there is no doubt that future scientists with more powerful tools will find smaller and smaller things inside today's seemingly smallest particles.

Space is everywhere; all objects, no matter how big or small, have volumetric space. When scientists explore the universe inside the atom, they find particles flying around in micro space. It is hard to imagine, but all objects consist mostly of space. Theoretically, no matter how small something is, there can always be something smaller, so it is theoretically possible for an unlimited number of things to exist inside of something, and it is theoretically possible for an unlimited amount of space to exist inside of all objects. There are no boundaries or edges to the universe, big or small. The physical universe cannot be pinned down.

This inexactness can be experienced in everyday life. One of my first jobs was to make a detailed drawing of a machine part. I was challenged with understanding dimensions and tolerances. My assignment was to draw and dimension a specific part that had to fit within an assembly of other parts. The specification required the part to be ten inches long, so I put a dimension on the drawing that read 10 inches. To my surprise, my supervisor said that the required dimension was 10.000 inches. I argued that those were equal dimensions. Ten is ten and zero is zero, so why did it matter how many zeros were to the right of the decimal point? Just mark off exactly ten inches and cut the part there.

That was when I learned there is no such thing as exactly ten inches or exactly any dimension. All we can do is make one thing close to the size of another thing. The more intricate and precise the machine, the smaller the tolerances need to be. When we get close enough, we consider the difference acceptable, but it can never be exact.

It took me some time to fully grasp the whole measurement concept. My problem was not in understanding the reasons for the relationship between dimensions and machining practices—I was having a much more basic problem. My scientific concept of the universe had led me to believe that our physical reality is made of standalone objects that exist with exact shapes and sizes independent of humanity. Therefore I had expected that designing and detailing objects would just be a matter of putting on paper what they actually are. Instead, the whole process turned out to be dependent on the way we humans interpret our world.

Measurement units such as "foot" and "meter" are distances that were arbitrarily established by someone many centuries ago. Measurement units originally varied greatly from place to place, because there was no reason for people from different geographical areas to see and do things the same way. This changed when populations expanded into each other, and standardized measurement systems were needed, developed, and spread throughout the civilized world.

The old arbitrary lengths have become today's standards. A standard "foot" and other standard units are always kept at the National Institute of Standards and Technology. These standard lengths are made of the most stable metals and stored in an environmentally conditioned room, because metals will expand or shrink depending on the temperature. Copies can be made from these masters and taken for use elsewhere.

Absolute dimensions do not exist. All measurements are based on comparisons to these standard but arbitrary lengths of metal, which are related to human body parts. The foot unit of measurement is a relationship and not an independently existing length of free space.

A draftsman can mark off two points on a piece of paper and then subdivide the space between the points in an unlimited number of smaller increments. You can call a length of space an inch or a mile or any arbitrary unit of length, because space is a relationship and not an absolute size. Two points in so-called free space have an unlimited amount of space between them, because space is not a freestanding thing.

If you were alone in space, you would have no knowledge of any other thing, so your size could not be calculated. In fact, you would not be able to describe anything except in relation to yourself. The length of your body would be approximately six times as long as your foot, but how big is six feet in relation to your universe? You would have no way of knowing whether you were as big as the whole universe or only a tiny part of it. All other physical attributes and measurements would likewise be undetermined.

During my studies it was becoming clear to me that space is not a freestanding volume. It is something that is generated by human interaction within the object world. A way to understand that space is not freestanding is to conduct a thought experiment. Imagine two identical spheres floating stationary in space. Then try to independently define how much distance there is between them. There is no way to determine the distance, except by comparing the space between the spheres to the size of the spheres. Picture in your mind the distance from center to center is about four times the spheres' diameters. Now imagine shrinking the spheres to half of their original diameters without changing their locations. The distance between the centers changes to eight times their diameter. It would seem like the spheres moved twice the distance apart. You can arrive back at the original picture by moving the half-sized spheres toward each other until the distance between their centers is again four times their diameters. This thought experiment shows how the sizes, volumes, and dimensions of objects and space are dependent on how we humans interpret what we sense.

This thought experiment is relevant to understanding the real world around us. Imagine the spheres to be as large as planets and that you are standing on the surface of one of them. You can see the other planet in one direction, but your sight and awareness of space is unlimited in all directions. It doesn't matter whether your planet is stationary or revolving around a sun. Space is not a fixed volume. Space is as big as you perceive it to be. You are at the center of your reality. You are at the center of a universe that is not fixed or infinite, but unlimited because of human imagination.

I wondered how space, objects, and gravity are related, and how it all is scientifically connected to humanity. Playing with rockets when I was a child made me start thinking about space and gravity and how it is possible for objects to be in orbit around Earth. Gravity seems very mysterious, but its action is easily defined. A gravitational field affects all things. All things have an attractive force associated with them that is directly proportional to the mass of the thing.

Newton's universal equation for the force of gravity is $F = Gmm/4\pi r^2$. This equation fits with real world experience, so it is valid for any universe model, freestanding or not. The force of gravity is small for small objects. For example it is hard to measure the gravitational force between two human bodies because the force is negligible. But when large amounts of small particles are combined to create a very large object such as our world, the accumulated force of gravity becomes very large, so the gravity of something very large strongly accelerates the small things around it.

The earth's gravity is the dominant force in our everyday world. As something gets larger, its surface area increases by the square of the radius, but its volume increases by the cube of the radius, so a large object has much more mass compared to its surface area. Since gravity is directly proportional to mass, the larger the object, the stronger the surface gravity.

Air molecules are held to the surface of the earth by gravity the same way humans, water, rocks, and everything else is held to the earth by gravity. The pressure of air is highest at ground level because the pull of gravity causes the air above to weigh down on and compress the air below.

If you weigh the air above a one-square-inch area of ground, you will find that it weighs approximately 14.7 pounds. This is the air pressure in which we humans live. We have almost fifteen pounds of force pressing on every square inch of our body's surface, so we have tens of thousands of pounds of force pressing in on our bodies at all times. Air pressure varies depending on altitude and weather conditions. The higher up from the ground we go, the less dense the air is, until there are no air molecules and therefore no pressure. If we were to go above the air (into outer space) without a compensating pressure suit, our bodies would expand and our blood would boil, because there is pressure inside of us and no counteracting pressure outside of us.

A vacuum is the absence of matter particles, so outer space is objectless and a vacuum. We think of space as being located far above the earth and beyond our atmosphere, but space is everywhere. All objects take up space. We take up space. Air molecules take up space. The earth takes up space. Atoms take up space. We humans move through the space that surrounds the earth's surface. Rockets must orbit above the atmosphere because they would otherwise heat up, slow down, and crash due to the friction of plowing through air molecules.

On the moon there is no atmosphere. Outer space is at ground level. An object could be put into orbit directly above the highest part of the moon's surface.

It is a misconception that there isn't any gravity in outer space. The earth is eight thousand miles in diameter, but almost the entire atmosphere is contained within less than one hundred miles above the ground. So if the earth were the size of a basketball, the atmosphere would be only a small fraction of an inch thick. In other words, a typical spacecraft orbiting at a hundred miles or so above the earth is only skimming the surface, so there is little difference in the force of gravity between the earth's surface and an orbiting spaceship.

Gravity's reach is unlimited out into space, and its strength diminishes with the square of the distance, according to Newton's universal equation. Astronauts appear to be weightless only because the spacecraft and the astronauts are traveling horizontally and falling around the earth. The very high angular velocity of an orbiting craft allows it to fall without hitting the ground. Einstein was one of the first to realize that you would get the same weightless sensation if you were in an elevator and the supporting cable broke. You would float weightless in the elevator cage (until it hit the bottom of the elevator shaft). Einstein realized there is no difference between being accelerated downward by gravity and being accelerated upward in an elevator. A human cannot tell the difference. It is the same phenomenon.

Galileo discovered that all objects in a vacuum regardless of their sizes or shapes or weights fall at the same rate. It doesn't matter whether the objects are also in horizontal motion or not. Suppose you are on the moon, where there is no atmosphere, and something is dropped from the height of a cannon barrel at the same time a cannonball is fired horizontal to the ground. If the ground is flat, the dropped object and the fired cannonball will hit the ground at the same time. The velocity of the cannonball will determine how far it will travel during the time it takes gravity to pull both objects down to the ground.

But like all massive objects in the universe, the moon's surface is not flat. It is shaped like a sphere, because gravity pulls everything inward toward the center of mass. The moon's surface is round and curves down and away from a horizontal line projected from the center of the cannon barrel.

According to Newton's laws of motion, all objects put into motion will travel in a straight line if there is an absence of force. Without gravitational force, the cannonball would not curve with the ground; it would go straight into outer space. The Moon does have gravity, however; if the cannonball's velocity is too low, gravity will pull it to the ground before it can make it over the horizon. If the cannonball is moving too fast, gravity cannot pull it down quickly enough, and it will travel a curved path into outer space. Even so, gravity's long reach will eventually slow it down and force it back to the moon's surface.

If the cannonball's velocity is just right, the distance the ball falls due to gravity will exactly match the distance the ground curves away, and the ball will maintain a constant distance at the height of the cannon barrel above the moon's surface. There is only one specific velocity that will work for any given orbital height. With no air resistance, the cannonball will maintain its orbit indefinitely. If you could shrink yourself and ride on or inside the cannonball, you would experience the sensation of being weightless, but gravity is still present and as strong as ever.

Many of us have experienced sub-orbital weightlessness without realizing it. When I was a young boy, my dad took my family to the country, where he knew the roads very well. One particular road had many small but steep hills. When we approached one particular hill, Dad sped up and said, "Hang on because you might hit your head on the roof." Sure enough, when we flew over the hill, we floated up and bumped our heads against the roof of the car. As we continued down the hill, we became suspended above our seats in total weightlessness. We made Dad do it a couple more times, and at just the right speed we went over the hill weightless but did not hit our heads.

I worked for a major aircraft manufacturing company during the Mercury, Gemini, and Apollo spacecraft programs in the 1960s. The astronauts came to this facility for training. Many of my coworkers were convinced that scientists and engineers had invented a gravity-free chamber to simulate the conditions of an orbiting spacecraft, but this is not true. We did have a vacuum chamber to simulate a near-zero atmosphere, but gravity penetrated the chamber just as it does everything else in the universe. Creating a vacuum is easy. All you have to do is pump the air out of the chamber. But it was hard to convince my friends that gravity is always everywhere and scientists don't know what it is or how to control it.

The way the early astronauts trained for weightlessness is the same way they still train today. A transport plane with a padded interior is flown in a parabolic arc in the sky. As the plane flies over the top of the arc, the astronauts float inside the plane just like I floated in my dad's car. The difference is that the transport plane flies in a much bigger arc at a much faster speed, and therefore the people inside the plane experience a much longer weightless time. In the case of an orbiting space ship, the arc becomes greater than the earth's radius, the velocity becomes around 17,500 miles per hour (depending on the height above the earth), and a permanent Earth orbit is achieved.

We can identify with gravity because it is the dominant force that we personally interact with. We even know how to measure gravity ourselves. When we get on the scales to see how much we weigh, we are measuring the downward pull of gravity. One hundred fifty pounds in weight is one hundred fifty pounds of force. Weight is another name for the force of gravity.

Our reality seems much more mysterious when we talk about atoms, electrons, and the flow of electricity. Even in science and engineering, there are two different fields of study for these two extremes in nature. Our visible macro-world is mechanical. Our invisible micro-world is electrical.

Gravity holds large things like planets together and provides the force to keep the objects in macro-reality functioning smoothly, but the gravity inherent in small objects is insignificant. Science has determined that a different force rules micro-reality. Electromagnetic forces provide the glue that allows nature to form small things, and these forces make it possible for the micro-world to function. Scientists are having the same problem with electromagnetism as they are with gravity, however. They understand how it acts, but they don't understand what it is or where it comes from.

In the late seventeenth century Newton discovered that the gravitational force diminishes inversely proportional to the square of the distance from the object's center of mass. In the late eighteenth century Charles Coulomb discovered that the electric force also diminishes inversely proportional to the square of the distance. But Coulomb discovered that, according to Newton's formula, the gravitational force associated with an atomic particle is many times weaker than the electrical force associated with the same particle. So the two forces are assumed to be disassociated phenomena. No one in science has ever found a connection.

Gravity and electricity must be connected, because the big and small parts of our reality are parts of the same continuous physical cosmos. Matter is matter, no matter how small it is. The particles in the atomic world are parts of the physical object world, even though they are too small to be seen. Everything—regardless of size—is made up of matter. The universe consists of objects being pushed, pulled, assembled, and disassembled in the continual process of changing and reshaping into something new, and the forces of nature are the glues that tie it all together.

A few years ago I was thinking about space, gravity, and matter while on a night flight coming back from a long and tiring business trip. I knew from Newton's universal law of gravitation that all objects have gravity and that gravitational force diminishes proportional to the square of the distance from the object, $F = Gmm/4\pi r^2$. I also remembered from Newton's second law of motion that when an object accelerates through space it encounters a resistance force from space, $F = ma$.

Let's use some logic. We know there is a resistance force exerted on an object by space when the object is accelerated through space. It follows that space would exert a like force on an object when space is accelerated past the object. I suddenly realized that objects are accelerated toward the earth, because space is flowing from outer space and down into the earth and into the interior of all objects that make up the earth. Space is flowing downward from outer space into the depths of the smallest pieces of known matter.

I wondered what is happening when space continues to accelerate inside the atom. I thought maybe atomic particles are actually constructed of accelerating space like a tornado is made of accelerated air or a whirlpool is made of accelerated water. It also occurred to me that the continuous downward flow from outer space to sub-atomic space would connect all of the forces of nature. I worked with Newton's equations to find out if this could be true.

$F = ma = Gmm/4\pi d^2$. Solving for mass, $m = G4\pi d^2 a = G4\pi d^3/t^2$. Since G is a gravitational constant that is only necessary to adjust for units, then $m = d^3/t^2$. Newton's equations show mass is accelerating volumetric space. This equation for mass is the same as in the supreme being's second proposal (physical from nonphysical, matter creation process). To my surprise, the secret of matter was right under Newton's nose hundreds of years ago. Could it be that scientists have been trained to expect something different? They have been so busy looking for a non-existing smallest fundamental piece of matter that they have ignored the real evidence. Unfortunately, modern science is stuck in a self-inflicted freestanding universe paradigm.

CHAPTER FIVE

How Science Went Down the Wrong Road

Humanity would be much better off if there had been a continued scientific evolution instead of a scientific revolution. Scientists would have continued to discover and transform our material world, but we would also have kept our God and our souls. We would now have the advantage of modern technology coupled with purpose in life, but that did not happen. Now, even with new evidence, it is hard for established science to change course.

Modern scientists have been immersed throughout their schooling and professional careers in the belief that our reality stands alone, disconnected from us, so they cannot think any other way. The freestanding paradigm is so imbedded in our modern culture that even the average citizen has a hard time believing the physical world is connected to human thought, but it is true. The facts are convincing.

We can find the beginnings of today's false scientific world-view thousands of years ago, when ancient cultures started to think critically about what things are made of and how things exist. A trip through the history of science and Western culture will expose how today's dead-end paradigm came about. At first there were many creation stories about the origin of the cosmos. Some viewed the process of creation as something that happened in the distant past. Others believed creation to be a continuing cycle of birth and destruction with no beginning and no end. There was no understanding of the mechanics of nature, so nothing was predictable. It was believed that one God or many gods were arbitrarily controlling the universe.

The various ancient cultures had small and different pictures of the universe, because they were scattered, with each people group living in isolation. They viewed reality from different geographical locations and therefore developed their own unique descriptions of the universe. These isolated cultures saw themselves as an integral part of their reality. Their physical connection to the material world gave them influence on their surroundings and made them susceptible to influence from their surroundings. They were big fish in a small pond. Each group developed its own physical interpretation of creation and intuitively believed in a larger unseen universe where humans go after death.

In the ancient human world, the cosmos was not seen as an independent thing that could be interpreted in only one true way; therefore, self-evident world-views could coexist. Then, as people began to settle in cities and civilizations grew and spread into each other's territories, world-views began to clash. People tend to believe that the things they see and experience are true, so without a common viewpoint, a single universe, with attributes that everyone could agree on, could not be determined.

Our Western culture has its roots in the land around the Mediterranean Sea. The first settlements were at the crossroads of Southern Europe, Southwest Asia, and North Africa in what is now called the Middle East. In this ancient world, religion enveloped all aspects of human life. Everything was part of the same process, which included activities such as science and medicine. We modern people now consider these as secular activities, because we have separated ourselves from the natural world around us.

Humans have always had the ability to study and modify their environment. Innovation has occurred throughout human history. But the reality for groups of hunter-gatherers was small. Change was slow and mostly limited to the needs of survival. The first innovations were simple tools and weapons. More advanced innovations would come with larger, more advanced cultures.

Humans began farming about twelve thousand years ago. Growing food was the beginning of the end of the nomadic life-style. The civilization of humanity eventually produced people who had more time and motivation to explore and to more closely study their surrounding universe.

By the tenth century BC, astronomers in Mesopotamia were mapping the stars in the night sky. They noticed that the stars were grouped to form shapes, which they called constellations. These constellations dotted the sky in a narrow belt called the zodiac (it was later realized this belt was our own galaxy). Names were given to each of the star groupings, some of which are still used today. Five visible stars moved relative to the background of fixed stars. These moving stars were called wandering stars or planets, because they moved individually from constellation to constellation. The paths of these planets were plotted as they wandered amongst the fixed stars.

Astronomers noticed that the planets sometimes moved ahead with respect to the stars, but sometimes they reversed and made retrograde loops. There was no physical explanation for this motion. In ancient times, people thought that celestial events, especially planetary motions, were connected with their own lives and fortunes. This belief, called astrology, encouraged the development of mathematical schemes for predicting the planetary motions and thus furthered the progress of astronomy.

Anaximenes, a Greek philosopher, claimed in the sixth century BC that air is the primary element of which everything is made. He introduced the concepts of condensation and rarefaction, which he thought explained how solid objects are formed. Anaximenes claimed these processes turned invisible air into water, fire, and solid matter. He thought that air became warmer, was rarefied, and turned to fire. He thought that air became colder, was condensed, and turned to solids. Obviously, we now know that his cosmology was wrong, but his attempt to discover the ultimate nature of reality has been the goal of scientists up to the present time.

Maps of the constellations were made by several ancient cultures including the Babylonians, the Chinese, the Mayans, and the Egyptians, but the Babylonians achieved the most success. They studied the motions of the sun and the moon to perfect their calendar. The day after a new moon, when the lunar crescent first appears after sunset, was the beginning of a month.

At first this lunar cycle was determined by observation, but by 400 BC they wanted to predict it in advance. Astronomers noticed that the motions of the sun and moon do not have a constant speed through the zodiac. The sun and moon move with increasing speed for the first half of their journeys and then decrease in speed during the last half. A mathematical method was developed to approximate this motion. With this mathematical model, Babylonian astronomers were able to predict the day on which the new moon would begin. This mathematical understanding allowed them to know in advance the positions of the sun and moon for every day of the month.

Our ancestors began to build cities and towns. The cradle of civilization was in Mesopotamia, between the Tigris and Euphrates rivers, where there was rich farmland in what is now modern-day Iraq. The Sumerians developed the first true civilization in this area of the world between 3500 BC and 1800 BC. They developed cities, writing, and much more. The wheel was invented sometime between 3500 BC and 3000 BC.

The Sumerians produced the world's first bronze. These people were the first to learn how to take nature's basic elements and combine them to form human-made metal products. The Sumerians also began to develop some of the first units of measure. Our modern use of the number twelve as applied to time and degrees and the dozen as a common unit of measure have their origins in this earliest of all civilizations.

Many different civilizations sprang up, only to be invaded and conquered by stronger civilizations. Civilization eventually spread throughout the Mediterranean area. The Old Kingdom of Egypt existed between 3100 BC and 2200 BC. The Egyptians were the first to use a single symbol to represent ten things. The old way was to make a separate mark for every object counted, so it would take one hundred marks to represent one hundred things. The new innovation was to use ten symbols to represent one hundred things. This was much better and was the beginning of our modern numbering system. These and many other mathematical and technological advances spread throughout the Mediterranean area.

The Mycenaean civilization was the first culture to dominate Greece. They populated Greece beginning around 2000 BC and spoke an early version of the Greek language. After dominating the area for many centuries, they fell into decline around 1200 BC. Their decline was probably due to being invaded by tribes from the north and east.

Civilization in this area of the world ceased to exist for many centuries. This uncivilized time was the archaic period of Greek history, which lasted from about 1200 BC until 500 BC. Even writing and art were lost until a new Greek civilization arose and began looking at things in a different way. The Greeks combined geometry with logic and created a system of thought that took mankind away from the limited view of personal experiences and toward what they thought were general truths about the universe.

In the sixth century BC Thales struggled with the questions of what things are made of and where matter comes from in the first place. He knew that these questions had to be answered in order to understand the universe and humanity's role in it.

Greek culture was at its peak between 500 BC and 336 BC. This is what is now called the classical Greek period, when Socrates, Plato, and Aristotle lived. These men had the most profound influence on the way the people of all modern cultures think.

Socrates lived in the Greek city of Athens between approximately 470 BC and 400 BC. He spent most of his life in public places engaging in dialogue and arguing with anyone who would engage with him. He believed in a purely objective understanding of the concepts of justice, love, virtue, and self-knowledge. Socrates taught people to think for themselves and to take nothing for granted. He wanted everyone to always question everything.

During the time of Socrates there were many philosophers who proposed many theories about the universe, like the shape or motion of the earth, the size of the sun, or the distance to the sun. But Socrates believed that even if humans could determine these things about the universe, it would make no difference in how they lived their lives. He believed that understanding the material world was not as important as understanding the nonmaterial eternal world of the soul that lay beyond the world of the senses.

Socrates thought that what we do need to know is how to conduct our own lives. What is good? What is just? He believed that things like goodness and justice actually existed, but he thought they did not decay and disappear like the objects we can experience; therefore they were eternal, and their existence was a nonmaterial essence. He believed that if people preserved their integrity, no real harm could be done to them. Unjust acts, crippling accidents, and diseases were chance happenings in an existence that is brief. From Socrates we learn that real personal tragedy is in the degradation of the soul. He never wrote anything down, but he had a great influence on his pupil Plato, who did.

Plato investigated the difference between the uncertain reality of the senses and universal truths, which he thought could be found only through rational thought. He was the first to use the term "philosophy," meaning, "love of knowledge." Plato was convinced of two essential characteristics of knowledge: first, he believed that knowledge must be certain and infallible; second, knowledge must have as its objective that which is genuinely real, as contrasted with that which is an appearance only. At the foundation of his ideas was his theory of forms, which claimed that "objects in the physical world merely resemble perfect forms in the ideal world, and that only these perfect forms can be the objects of true knowledge."

Like Socrates, Plato believed in both the physical and the nonphysical worlds, but he believed that the key to understanding the universe lay in understanding mathematics and physics. He thought that every single thing in nature was a decaying copy of something whose ideal form had a permanent and indestructible existence outside space and time.

Plato saw the universe as being divided into two realms: the visible world that we can sense, and another part of the universe not existing in space and time and imperceptible to the eye. According to Plato, our physical space-and-time world is the only world our sensory apparatus can apprehend, but it is the one where nothing lasts and nothing stays the same. The not-in-space-and-time realm is inaccessible to our senses, so it is the one where there is permanence and perfect order. Plato thought it should be called the real reality, because it alone is permanent. Plato taught that our physical bodies come into existence and then soon pass away, but they are brief impressions of the nonmaterial, timeless, and indestructible "us" that we call our soul. He thought that the only harm that could come to a person is harm to the permanent soul, so he thought it was far better in the long run for a person to suffer wrong than to do wrong.

Plato founded the academy of Athens, considered the first European university, in 387 BC. A wide range of subjects—such as astronomy, mathematics, biology, political theory, and philosophy—could be learned there. Plato's influence through the history of philosophy has been monumental. He had a large impact on all major religions, and his ideas have played a central role in Christian theology. Plato also had a famous student who went on to have an even greater impact on the future of the world than his teacher. The student's name was Aristotle.

Aristotle was a Greek philosopher and scientist born in Macedonia in 384 BC. He went to Athens, where he studied and taught in Plato's academy for twenty years—until Plato's death. Then he returned to Macedonia, where he tutored Alexander, the king's son, who was to succeed his father as ruler. After Alexander took the throne, Aristotle returned to Athens and established his own school, where he taught until his death in 322 BC. As king, Alexander's exploits were so successful and far-reaching that he became known as Alexander the Great.

Aristotle had Plato's reverence for human knowledge but revised many of his ideas. Aristotle focused on methods based on observation and experience. He researched and organized most branches of knowledge and made available the first ordered disciplines of physics, biology, psychology, and literary theory. Aristotle also created formal logic and zoology, and he addressed every major philosophical problem known at the time. He is most likely the greatest thinker in Western history and probably had the greatest influence on Western intellectual development.

Aristotle's philosophy was based on biology, as opposed to Plato's mathematics and physics. Aristotle viewed the world as consisting of individual things, where each thing has a built-in pattern of development and grows toward self-realization. He considered growth, purpose, and direction to be built into all individual substances. Aristotle's idea of causality was most important. He explained that each thing has more than one reason that helps to explain what, why, and where it is.

Past Greek philosophers had thought that only one cause could be explanatory. Aristotle had four causes. The material cause was the matter out of which a thing is made. The efficient cause was the source of motion, generation, or change. The formal cause was the species, kind, or type. The final cause was the goal, or full development, of an individual, or the intended function of a construction or invention.

Aristotle defined a finite, spherical universe, with a motionless earth at its center. He further defined the earth as consisting of four elements—earth, air, fire, and water—and said that each of these four elements had a proper place, determined by its relative heaviness or specific gravity. Aristotle believed that each element moved naturally in a straight-line: earth down, fire up, toward its proper place, where it would be at rest. He thought terrestrial motion was always linear through a resistive medium and therefore always came to a halt.

Aristotle believed the heavens must be made of a fifth and different element he called the ether, which was a superior element and incapable of any change other than change of place in a circular movement. He claimed that heavier bodies of a given material fell faster than lighter ones when their shapes were the same. This was a mistaken view that was not corrected until Galileo conducted his experiment with balls rolling down an inclined plane.

Aristotle was the first to use the term "metaphysics," which is the branch of philosophy concerned with the ultimate nature of reality. He believed that a divine being he referred to as the "prime mover" was responsible for the unity and purposefulness of nature. He believed in a perfect God and that all things desired to share God's perfection.

Aristotle's greatest strength was his ability to reconcile opposing views with his rational discussions. He was able to convince everyone that his ideas were the truth because he was able to give logical, commonsense explanations for the composition of matter, the movements of objects in the sky surrounding the earth, the role of mankind, and the perfection of heaven.

The people of the Aristotelian period were sure they knew everything that could be known. It was believed that anything they did not know was God's work and could not be known by humans. Therefore, nothing was left to discover.

Aristotle rejected Plato's two-world theory. He did not believe in an abstract realm independent of space and time, where ideal forms reside, accessible only to the intellect. He believed that the world we live in and sense is the only world that means anything to us. He thought that, as far as we are concerned, it is the only one that does exist, and anything outside of possible experience would be unreliable and therefore could be nothing for us. He believed that only one world could be confidently talked about. It is this ever-changing world of the senses we live in, according to Aristotle, and it is possible to determine reliable knowledge from it.

Aristotle admitted that the question of how things exist and what is being is very difficult to answer. But he was not a strict materialist. He believed that a thing is whatever it is, by virtue of its nonmaterial form, but that form does not come from another world. Form is that which causes a thing to be what it is. Form is the explanation of things.

Aristotle thought that an object's form was inherent in the object and could not exist separately from it. He believed that by understanding how something acted, we could arrive at an understanding of what it is. He believed things are simply here.

Aristotle's teachings coupled with his far-reaching influence have shaped the modern perception of the universe.

He did not, however, address Thales' question about the mystery of matter, so the world went forward, albeit without a true understanding of how the universe exists. Subsequently variations of both Plato's and Aristotle's philosophical approaches have become competing foundations for many religious world-views. These two philosophers have put forth the main two opposing philosophical approaches that have continued throughout history even to this day. On one side are philosophers and theologians who put little value on knowledge of this world of the senses and believe that our ultimate concern should be with the world that lies beyond the sensed world. On the other side there are the philosophers and scientists who believe that this sensed world is the only object of our concern.

The Aristotelian universe model dominated for nearly two thousand years. The influence of Aristotle's philosophy is everywhere in Western culture. It has even helped to shape modern language and common sense. His doctrine of the prime mover as final cause has played an important role in theology.

Until the twentieth century, logic meant Aristotle's logic. Until the Renaissance and even later, astronomers, scientists, and poets have admired his concept of the universe. Zoology was based on Aristotle's work until Charles Darwin modified the doctrine of the non-changing of species in the nineteenth century. A new admiration for Aristotle's method and its application to education, literary criticism, and political analysis developed during the twentieth century

CHAPTER SIX

The Emergence of the Modern Freestanding Model

As the Macedonian king, Alexander ruled all of Greece, as had his father, King Philip II. Alexander went on to conquer most of the civilized world. In 333 BC he conquered Asia Minor, Syria, and then Egypt. Then he conquered Babylon and the Persian army. At the age of thirty-three he died, the finest general the world had ever known. During his reign Greek culture reached regions as far away as India, Persia, and Mesopotamia. Alexander's empire broke up after his death, and regional rulers set up independent kingdoms. One of the largest of these was the Ptolemaic kingdom of Egypt.

Greek tradition took hold most firmly in Egypt, where Alexander established a new capital, which he named Alexandria. It was a city of large buildings, dominated by the Pharos, a lighthouse standing more than 440 feet tall. Alexandria also boasted a library housing nearly 500,000 scrolls.

The Greeks continued to excel in the arts and sciences during what later came to be called the Hellenistic age, between 336 BC and 27 BC. Meanwhile the Romans were building an empire to the northwest in southern Europe. Rome rose between the years 755 BC and 44 BC.

The Greek mathematicians took ideas of mathematics from the Babylonians and the Egyptians. The difference in Greek mathematics was the invention of an abstract mathematics founded on a logical structure of definitions, axioms, and proofs. This development started in the sixth century BC with Thales of Miletus and Pythagoras of Samos. Pythagoras taught the importance of studying numbers in order to understand the world. Early Greeks calculated pi, which is the ratio between the diameter of a circle and its circumference, to roughly 3 1/7. One of the great mathematicians of the fifth century BC was the philosopher Democritus of Abdera. It was he who discovered the correct formula for the volume of a pyramid.

Euclid was a mathematician and teacher who worked at the Museum of Alexandria. Around 300 BC, he wrote thirteen books called the *Elements*. They contained much of the basic mathematical knowledge discovered up to the end of the fourth century BC on the geometry of polygons and the circle, the theory of numbers, the theory of incommensurables, solid geometry, and the theory of areas and volumes. *Elements* is still one of the most frequently translated and studied books in the world. Euclid established a mathematical foundation that students still follow to this day. Euclid's mathematics assigns fixed dimensions and values, including areas and volumes, to the object world. This helps reinforce the perception that the universe stands alone and separate from us in space and time.

The century after Euclid was filled with mathematical brilliance. Archimedes of Syracuse theoretically weighed infinitely thin slices to find the areas and volumes of figures arising from conic sections. Archimedes also investigated centers of gravity and various solids floating in water. His work paved the way for the invention of calculus by Newton and Leibniz in the seventeenth century. Archimedes was killed by a Roman soldier during the sack of Syracuse.

Archimedes' younger contemporary Apollonius produced an eight-book treatise that established the ellipse, parabola, and hyperbola, which are the names of the conic sections. This work was the foundation of geometry until French philosopher and scientist René Descartes further advanced mathematics in the seventeenth century. The mathematical advances of Apollonius gave Greek astronomers the tools they needed to solve the problems of spherical astronomy and to develop an astronomical system that dominated until the time of the German astronomer Johannes Kepler.

Alexander's empire began breaking up by the end of the third century BC due to insurrection and rebellion. Macedonia was finally subdued by the Roman Empire in 148 BC after several wars, and Macedonia became a province. Rome defeated the Ptolemies in Egypt in 30 AD, which ended the Hellenistic kingdoms, but Hellenistic culture continued to survive; its influence is felt to this very day. Rome defeated the Greeks, but the Romans were so impressed with Greek culture that its fine art and literature were transported back to Rome.

Imperial Rome dominated the civilized world from 44 BC to 476 AD. Julius Caesar conquered the lands once controlled by Alexander, but Caesar did not stop there. He extended the Roman Empire to the north as far as Great Britain. Caesar and his army became so powerful that he began to threaten Rome itself. After conquering Britain, he went back to fight for total control. Caesar chased his enemies into Greece and Egypt, where his army burned the great library of Alexandria. This loss of this literature is one of the greatest tragedies in the history of Western civilization.

Ptolemy was a philosopher, mathematician, and astronomer born sometime around 170 AD. He lived in Alexandria when the Romans ruled Egypt and Alexandria was the center of Greek culture. Ptolemy's most well-known book is the *Almagest*. In this book Ptolemy proposed a theory that mathematically defined the positions and motions of the planets, sun, and moon against a background of fixed stars.

Ptolemy's theory began with the widely held belief of the time that the earth does not move and is at the center of the universe. This seemed like common sense to someone standing on the massive earth and looking up into the sky, seeing the much smaller sun and moon. The vast distances between them were unknown, so no one realized that adjustments of size for distance should be made. For philosophical purposes, the planets and stars were considered to move in perfect orbits. Ptolemy complicated his theory in an attempt to solve astronomical mysteries that could not otherwise be accounted for in an earth-centered system, such as the backward motions of the planets and the variations in size or brightness of the moon and planets. He theorized that the planets, sun, and moon all move in small circles around much larger earth-centered circles. In this way he made his theory fit most recorded astronomical observations, which at that time were not very accurate, because they were made with the naked eye.

Ptolemy's common-sense, earth-centered theory was believed to be true for fifteen hundred years. It was unquestioned until Copernicus proposed his sun-centered theory. Even though the earth-centered system was in question, it was still maintained by scientists and the church alike until Galileo used his telescope to observe the workings of the solar system and prove the Copernican system right.

The Middle Ages was a time in European history between the disintegration of Rome and the beginning of the Renaissance, a period covering almost one thousand years. It is regarded as a period of decline bordered by two high civilizations, but the Middle Ages did achieve some progress. During this time the Christian church was the most powerful authority in Western civilization, and the stage was being prepared for the great achievements that were to come later in Renaissance Europe.

Aristotle and Ptolemy's works were lost in the West after the fall of Rome, but they were not lost in the East. During the Middle Ages, the Christian church taught that the earth was flat, immoveable, and at the center of everything. Later, during the ninth century, Arab scholars introduced Aristotle to the Islamic world. Then, in the twelfth century, Spanish-Arab philosopher Averroes studied and spread knowledge about Aristotle in the West.

By the thirteenth century the West's knowledge of Aristotle's work was renewed, and Saint Thomas Aquinas adopted it as a new philosophical foundation for Christian thought. At first church officials regarded Aristotle's philosophy as suspicious, because his teachings were thought to be a materialistic view of the world. Even so, Aquinas's adaption of Aristotle was accepted, and the scholastics developed a philosophical tradition that included the earth-centered cosmology of Ptolemy.

The Christian church adopted a cosmology based on the theories of Aristotle and Ptolemy because an earth-centered model closely matched common-sense observations at the time, and it placed humanity at the physical center of everything. This cosmological theory postulated a geocentric universe in which the earth was stationary and motionless at the center of several concentric, rotating spheres. These spheres bore the following celestial bodies from Earth outward: the Moon, Mercury, Venus, the Sun, Mars, Jupiter, and Saturn. The finite outermost sphere bore the so-called fixed stars.

The geocentric model posed a problem for scientists and theologians that had been difficult to explain since ancient times. Mars, Jupiter and Saturn sometimes appeared to halt and then proceed in the opposite direction. In an attempt to account for this retrograde or backward motion, medieval cosmology stated that each planet revolved on the edge of a circle called the epicycle and that the center of each epicycle revolved around the earth on a path called the deferent. As observations of the sky improved, this complicated and convoluted model could no longer sufficiently explain these mysterious motions. The adoption of Ptolemy's geocentric model had become a big liability for church doctrine, but church authorities were bound and determined to defend it.

In the fourteenth century, Italy's city-states became independent. This break from centralized rule encouraged individual freedom and prosperity, which in turn was the incubator for the Renaissance. Scholars became aware of long-forgotten Greek and Roman texts and were very impressed by them, so in some ways the Renaissance was a rebirth of ancient culture. Actually it brought about a new freedom of thought that caused an explosion in writing, art, and science rather than the re-introduction of former knowledge. The Renaissance was a completely new outlook on life that put more emphasis on the importance of individuality. The Renaissance in Europe marked the beginning of modern times.

The main roadblock to the emergence of modern science and the nonhuman model of the universe lay in the continued belief in a view of nature based on the ideas of Aristotle, Ptolemy, and Christian theologians: the view that the entire physical universe was centered on humankind and that there was a basic, God-given purpose to all movement. Gravity was explained as the preference for all bodies to be at the center of the earth. Acceleration was explained as a result of the increasing eagerness of a falling body as it fell closer and closer to its natural home. This interpretation of nature was still mostly supernatural and was not open to objective or experimental analysis.

The most important feature of Renaissance science was the introduction of the concept of the universe as something that could be studied objectively. The discoveries of Copernicus, Galileo, and Newton uncovered a cosmos more vast and complex than ever before imagined. New detailed measurements and mathematical relationships showed that Earth is only a small planet circling a minor star within one of billions of galaxies containing billions more stars. The Western picture of the cosmos changed from Earth being the biggest and most important object to Earth being a small and insignificant object, and so did we. Our relationship within our reality changed from humans being the main players to humans being very small in comparison to all that exists.

The spirit of the Renaissance encouraged individual curiosity and experimentation, which were the keys to the development of modern science. Experience was emphasized over abstract theory. Renaissance scientists tried to observe the natural world carefully and without preconceived ideas. There were scientific advances in many fields, but the apparent spirit of impartial inquiry had more influence on modern science than any particular scientific accomplishment.

The Renaissance spirit encouraged a stronger interest in the visible world, while it discouraged abstract speculations and interest in life after death. Christianity was not abandoned, but the religious dogma of the previous thousand years all but disappeared. Leonardo da Vinci represented the total Renaissance man—he was a sculptor, painter, engineer, architect, musician, scientist, and inventor. The Renaissance spirit in art was apparent in the representation of humanity and nature more realistically. Leonardo, Michelangelo, and Raphael's paintings of figures are fleshier and their landscapes more solid and three-dimensional.

The Renaissance spirit opened the universe to investigation and reinterpretation, but because the universe was still very mysterious, scientific discovery could not yet be separated from old philosophical ideas. There was no firm foundation for the new science to build on. Beginning in the fifteenth century, philosophers and scientists proposed many new systems of thought. Some were based on mechanistic, materialistic interpretations of the universe, while others were founded on a belief in human thought as the only ultimate reality. There was too little scientific evidence to determine which of these two main world-views was scientifically correct.

French mathematician René Descartes was a very influential, early seventeenth-century mathematician and philosopher. He followed the actions of Galileo by criticizing established methods and beliefs. Descartes determined that a human being is fundamentally a mind, and the only way that we can understand the universe is through rational thinking. He proposed a universe made of only two substances. He explained that in nature there are two kinds of entity: mind and matter, subject and object, and observer and observed. Descartes used mathematics as the model for all science and applied its deductive and analytical methods to all fields. His first major book, *Essais Philosophiques,* was published in 1637. Descartes would not believe anything, including his own existence, unless he could prove it to be true. He saw the logical proof of his own existence in the very act of questioning it. Descartes concluded, "Cogito ergo sum" ("I think, therefore I am"). This, he theorized, was how the existence of God and the basic laws of nature could be deduced.

Descartes further refined the new world-views of Copernicus and Galileo. He wanted to put all human knowledge on an absolute and certain foundation. He refused to believe anything unless it could be logically and scientifically seen, measured, and therefore proven. Even though he had a mechanistic view of the universe, Descartes believed in the traditional religious doctrine of the immortality of the soul. He maintained that mind and body are two distinct substances. By separating the mind from the mechanistic laws of nature, he was able to explain freedom of the will.

Descartes argued for a mind that is separate from the physical universe, including the physical body, but he never could adequately address the problem concerning how a nonphysical mind could affect and control a physical body. This is a problem he was unable to solve, and to this day it is one of the main concerns of philosophy. Neither was Descartes able to answer the question of what are things made of. Like Aristotle, he just assumed that physical things need nothing outside themselves in order to exist. While Descartes could not explain how the universe exists, he still believed that it had to be created in order to exist, and so he continued to believe in an abstract God.

Benedict Spinoza followed Descartes as an important and very influential seventeenth-century philosopher. He believed that we humans live in a cosmos where everything is included in a single substance that is God and therefore always under the influence of God's will. He claimed that our explanations always consist of connecting things to other things, so the totality of everything is the only thing that has nothing outside of itself. Mental and material are two different ways of seeing the same thing. He disputed Descartes' dualism by saying that if the universe consists of mental substances and material substances that are not connected, then how is it possible for the mind to connect to and move matter around in space and time? How can a mind control its human body?

Spinoza developed a theory of the universe where God is everywhere and is the cause of all things, so there is only one substance. He theorized that a human is a finite being with a body and a soul, but the soul is not separate; therefore the body and soul are the same thing and the same person. Spinoza explained that our religious interpretation of the universe and our scientific interpretation of the universe are both descriptions of the same totality, so there is no such thing as free will, because God controls everything.

John Locke was another famous seventeenth-century philosopher whose work is still admired in the present day. He believed that matter is an invisible substance that cannot be defined. He theorized that science can determine information about an object—such as its length, width, height, velocity, and position in space—because these attributes are independent of the observer. But he thought objects have characteristics that science cannot determine, such as taste and color, because these characteristics are a part of the interaction between the observer and the object and not inherent in the object. Some aspects of the objects change from one observer to another. So, he theorized, we can't know what an object is because we have no way of knowing it independent of its observable characteristics.

Locke realized that our senses are our only connection to external reality.

Isaac Newton was the most brilliant mathematician and physicist in world history. His life's work spanned the later seventeenth century and early eighteenth century, when he looked past the mysteries of the universe and put science on a firm mathematical foundation. His scientific laws gave people the impression that all things in space move strictly according to scientific laws. Newton was also a philosopher in his own right. He didn't think material things just simply exist or that things can come from nothing, so he believed that the universe had to have been originally created. But he thought that the universe is governed by strict laws of cause and effect, so God must have set everything in motion and left it to move through time in a deterministic manner.

Gottfried Wilhelm Leibniz must also be included as a very influential, latter seventeenth-century and early eighteenth-century mathematician and philosopher. Unlike the other philosophers, he developed a detailed theory on the nature of matter. He theorized that all objects in the universe are dots of consciousness that occupy points in space. Previous philosophers and scientists thought matter was inert and that a force had to be applied to set it into motion. He considered that motion or activity is inherent in matter, and the ultimate make-up of matter is a nonmaterial center of activity. Leibniz philosophized that God created the best possible world, which does contain free will. As a result there is wrongdoing and evil, but this is better than a world in which there is no free will.

George Berkeley was another important philosopher who continued the quest to understand the universe during the first half of the eighteenth century. He theorized that matter cannot be conceived to exist independent of the mind. He believed that minds and their contents are all that does exist, and there is no evidence that anything else exists, especially not independent matter. A deity that continually induces perception in the human mind is the only way to explain the phenomena of sense. Berkeley claimed that the being of sensed things consists in their being perceived. Other philosophers could not go along with Berkeley's conclusion that everything is in the mind and independent matter does not exist, because it seems obvious that each of us has an independent mind that is outside everyone else's mind.

Immanuel Kant was one of the most influential philosophers in history and the central figure in modern philosophy. Kant continued the search for understanding where Berkeley left off, in the latter half of the eighteenth century. Kant believed, as did Berkeley, that objects by themselves do not exist and that space and time exist only in the mind. But unlike Berkeley, he did not believe that everything exists only in the mind. He theorized that everything that exists makes up the total reality, which includes the sensed world, our souls, and God. But Kant did not believe, as did most past philosophers and scientists, that what does exist is the only limiting factor that determines what we can ever know. Therefore he thought that it is impossible to eventually discover everything that does exist. He believed that all that can be known of the universe is only that which people can actually sense.

Kant theorized that on one side is the "world of phenomena," which is the world of things as they appear to us and is the world of possible knowledge for us. On the other side is the "noumenal world," which is the world of things as they are in themselves and is the world we cannot access. Everything in the noumenal world is transcendental. It exists, but it cannot be experienced. The noumenal world is where free will takes place. Kant believed that physical objects are simply the material from which sensations are formed, so the physical world is unknowable. He believed that space and time are a part of the sensing process, and this space and time sensing process is the means by which we know what we perceive.

Johann Gottlieb Fichte was a late eighteenth-century and early nineteenth-century philosopher. Fichte was inspired by Kant, but he went even further in theorizing that the physical universe is a function of the mind. He believed that the physical universe is the creation of its observers. He believed, as did Kant, that scientific laws could not be logically derived from observations, but he thought that observations could be derived from scientific laws. Fichte believed Newton's physics to be absolute, so the events in the sensed world must play out in a certain way. Therefore, he said, the universe is a physical manifestation of our perception of it.

During the nineteenth century, scientists and philosophers continued to argue whether the universe existed inside the mind or whether it existed freestanding and separate from human consciousness. Some understood that we form a picture of the universe in our minds through our senses as information comes to us, so we do not actually see and know the universe outside our minds. It is a fact that space and time, and therefore solid objects, cannot be scientifically shown to exist, freestanding and separate from human consciousness. To these scientists and philosophers it was obvious that future scientists and philosophers should not separate the physical universe from humanity.

Other scientists and philosophers were concluding, based on personal philosophy and not scientific evidence, that the universe is a vast and overpowering entity that exists separate from the human mind. They theorized that the physical universe is a freestanding process with no religious purpose, that humanity is merely a highly evolved side attraction, and that the mind or soul has evolved along with and wholly contained within the human being. Unfortunately, the freestanding thinkers were beginning to dominate.

Early in the nineteenth century Georg Wilhelm Friedrich Hegel theorized that the universe is a unity defined as something in between material and spiritual, and it is always in a continuous process of change and development. Hegel thought that understanding this process brought self-awareness, which was the ultimate goal. His theory claimed that the process was made of a fundamental thing he called "geist," which was neither material nor spiritual. Geist, he claimed, was the essence of all being. Hegel further claimed that change comes from forces within the process, and we are caught up in the process and carried along with it, so we have no power to resist or affect what is happening to us. Hegel concluded that as society rises above the individual, the ideal state will be realized, and change and conflict will come to an end.

Hegel's influence on the direction of modern society has been enormous. His theory of the ideal state was instrumental in the rise of Adolph Hitler's Nazism and Karl Marx's communism. Marx adopted practically all of Hegel's philosophy except for what the universe is made of. Marx took the position that reality is neither mental nor spiritual but entirely material.

Most philosophers and scientists before Hegel thought that the universe was a constant assembly of things to be explained. But Hegel changed the direction of philosophy by suggesting that the universe is not a thing; it is an ongoing, changing process that can be understood by knowing what it is, how it got here, and what it's going to be. This was the change in thinking that encouraged Charles Darwin to develop his theory of evolution.

Arthur Schopenhauer was an influential philosopher who also did his work during the first half of the nineteenth century. Schopenhauer developed his philosophy by critiquing Kant's philosophy, theorizing that the entire cosmos is so vast and overpowering that it is impossible for us to conceive it. Therefore, he believed it could have no connection to our minds. Schopenhauer agreed that the universe is divided into the phenomenal and the noumenal worlds. But he could not agree that the noumenal world consists of things as they are in themselves, because in order to differentiate between things, space and time must be present, otherwise they could not be separated and would be one and the same.

Schopenhauer believed that the noumenal world could not consist of independent things like souls and free will and therefore cannot be the cause of the phenomenal world. Instead Schopenhauer believed that acts of will and body movements are one and the same event. He believed that the phenomenal and the noumenal are of the same reality, that the universe is without any purpose, and that compassion comes from the noumenal where, at the ground of our being, we are all one and the same.

Schopenhauer was the first Western philosopher to openly claim to be an atheist. The influence of his work has had an enormous impact on other philosophers and other famous and influential people throughout the nineteenth, twentieth, and into the twenty-first century.

The Industrial Revolution began in England and quickly spread to Europe and America. The first railroad was constructed in England in 1830 between Liverpool and Manchester. Thomas Edison's phonograph was introduced in 1877. The first automobile and George Eastman's box camera both appeared in 1885. The Wright Brothers proved men could fly when they made the first successful powered flight in 1903. The Industrial Revolution changed the world from consisting of agricultural societies to modern industrial societies. It put farmers in factories, created a global economy, and increased the living standard of the average person.

While the Industrial Revolution was changing the world, another world-changing revolution was taking place in the field of biology. Charles Darwin, a British scientist, developed the foundation of modern evolutionary theory with his concept that all forms of life developed through the process of natural selection. He began formulating his theory at the age of twenty-two when, against his father's wishes, he jumped at the chance to work aboard the English survey ship HMS *Beagle* on a scientific expedition around the world. This voyage gave Darwin the chance to observe many different geological formations as well as a large variety of species, fossils, and organisms found on different islands and continents.

Darwin was very impressed with the effects that natural forces have had on forming the Earth's surface. His observations of the variations in fossils, plants, and animals made him doubt that they were specially created. He saw that certain fossils of allegedly extinct species looked very similar to living species in the same geographical areas. He observed that each island in the Galapagos Islands maintained its own form of mockingbird, finch, and tortoise. The different forms were related but varied in structure and eating habits from island to island. Darwin's observations made him realize there was a possible link between distinct but similar species.

Charles Darwin's thinking was greatly influence by Hegel's philosophy. Darwin believed that the universe is constantly undergoing change and that humanity is caught up in the process as products of the change. Darwin's theory of evolution by natural selection states that because of the food supply problem, the young born to any species intensely compete for survival. Those young that survive to produce the next generation tend to embody favorable natural variations (the process of natural selection); these variations are passed on by heredity. Each generation improves adaptively over the preceding generations, and this gradual and continuous process is the source of the evolution of the species. Darwin also introduced the concept that all organisms are descended from a common ancestor.

Darwin's complete theory was published in 1859 in *On the Origin of Species*. His book is often referred to as "the book that shook the world." It has been a major influence on the life sciences and on modern thought in general.

Attacks on Darwin's ideas came not from scientists but from religious opponents. The thought that living things had evolved by natural processes apparently denied the special creation of humankind and seemed to place humanity on a plane with animals. Darwin's work challenged the existence of God.

Friedrich Nietzsche was a German philosopher who was very influential during the late nineteenth century, and his works are still admired to this day. He pronounced to the world that "God is dead" and "since there is no God, and no world other than this one, then morals, ethics, and values cannot be what is called transcendental; they cannot come to us from anywhere outside this world, for there is nowhere else."

Nietzsche believed there is no other world, no other life, and no purpose to anything beyond what we experience here. He followed in the footsteps of Schopenhauer by believing there is no such thing as God and there is no immortal soul. But unlike Schopenhauer, Nietzsche thought that what we see is all there is to reality, and we are subject to the will of irrational forces. Therefore he viewed life as meaningless and full of pointless suffering.

Nietzsche believed we should get everything we can out of life and live it to the maximum of our ability, because this is all there is for us. His philosophy is about how best to accomplish this goal in a meaningless universe. Happiness to Nietzsche meant self-fulfillment. His ideas have had considerable influence on our modern society.

Along the way many scientists and philosophers realized that space and matter cannot be proved to exist outside the mind, but a lack of scientific evidence has not stopped scientists from embracing a godless and anti-human freestanding universe model. History shows us that modern science is not built on a sound scientific foundation; rather it is a product of our philosophy. Unfortunately, modern scientists are still trying to define the universe as a freestanding physical system.

During the twentieth century and now in the twenty-first century, scientists have been trying to do something that is impossible. They have continued to try to scientifically define a universe separate from God and mankind. They have always failed and always will fail. They have failed to find an outer edge. They have failed to find an independent, indivisible, indestructible foundation (a smallest particle}. They have failed to unify the forces of nature. And they have failed to define what matter is or where it comes from. Why? Because the universe does not work the way they think it does.

Ironically, it is not hard to find evidence to support the human universe model. Modern science vastly underestimates the power of the human mind. Scientists admittedly know very little about it. Scientists do know that the human brain is the most complex thing in the known universe, but they are struggling to understand the concept of the mind and the thought process. It is a known scientific fact that we do not directly see things. We do not look out across space and see freestanding objects. We receive information from objects in the form of electromagnetic energy, and then we transform the information into a solid three-dimensional reality on our personal viewing screen. Light energy is either emitted from or reflected from something. This light then travels and strikes anything in its path such as an eye, where receptors are stimulated. These incoming electrical signals are conveyed to the brain. The brain then processes the information.

The senses of hearing, smell, touch and taste are also electrical signals that provide input to constructing our solid reality. So, our outer world is generated from an electrical information process. Nature's process is similar to (but much more sophisticated than) what we experience when we participate in a human-created virtual program. We transform nonphysical information into the solid world we live in.

Virtual reality is a recent invention that is made possible because of improvements in computer power and sensory technology. It differs from other computer simulations in that it requires special interface devices that transmit the sights, sounds, and sensations of the simulated world to the user. These devices also record and send the speech and movements of the participants to the simulated world. Virtual reality enables a user to move and react in a computer-simulated environment. Various types of devices allow users to sense and manipulate virtual objects much as they would real objects. This natural style of interaction gives participants the feeling of being immersed in the simulated world. A human participant in a virtual reality senses his or her environment as a real and solid world, but it is actually a programmed mathematical model. This sensing process translates to our real world.

Today's virtual computer power, mathematical programs, and sensory hookups are still primitive, so life-like three-dimensional modeling cannot yet be completely simulated. Also, participants cannot be totally immersed into the simulation, but computing power continues to increase and sensory devices are steadily improving. Sometime in the future virtual simulations will rival real world interactions. It will be possible for a participant's mind with a virtual body to be completely embedded in a virtual program, and it will be impossible for a participant to tell the difference between virtual and actual reality.

These experiences, including a person's virtual life form, only exist as solid objects in the mind of the participants embedded in the reality. Virtual reality shows that there really is a direct connection between a person's soul and his or her physical universe.

The mind processes virtual information in the same way that it processes real information, so our real reality fundamentally works the same way virtual reality works. All realities are made of things interacting with other things in space and time. A virtual scientist might discover our same laws and formulas of physics, depending on how the reality was programmed. If virtual microscopes were to be used to analyze the things in a virtual world, it would be discovered—as in our real reality—that all virtual objects are electrical in nature. A virtual world does not have physical boundaries. Like our real world, a virtual world can be scientifically explored and expanded without limits.

Physical evidence does not support the modern freestanding model. If our universe were freestanding, then scientists would be able to mathematically unify and define it. Physical evidence does support the human model, which mathematically defines and unifies the whole universe process. Analysis of the outer and inner edges of our reality shows it is consistent with the way an unlimited human cosmos would work. If the human mind converts virtual programmed information into a working solid reality, then the human mind must be doing the same thing when it generates our real reality. I believe past philosophers and scientists would have developed the human model instead of the freestanding model if they had known then what we know now.

Like Aristotle, today's scientists accept as real only that which can be sensed and measured, so they falsely assume we live in a freestanding universe disconnected from God and humanity. Unfortunately for humanity, modern science has been based on philosophy and not on science. The modern scientific model does not have a firm scientific foundation.

Scientific Theory of God: Proof that God Exists ~ John Michael Thompson

CHAPTER SEVEN

In the Center of Everything

Throughout history philosophers and scientists have thought about and probed the universe in an effort to understand how it works and define its structure. But all have struggled at the same two mysterious places— the outer edge of their known universe and the inner edge of their known universe.

Each generation has defined a largest outer radius and a smallest particle of matter as the boundaries of their freestanding world. What they did not understand during their time is that these boundaries were human perceptions and not real freestanding edges. Succeeding generations of scientists have always found more space and more material objects, big and small. And this trend is not ending.

Viewing nature with the naked eye formed our ancestors' reality. Even though our human knowledge of reality has changed tremendously since then, the size of the reality they saw with their naked eyes is the same size as the reality we modern humans now see with our naked eyes. We are designed with certain physical capabilities, and our eyes cannot distinguish individual particles smaller than a certain diameter. When we look at the details of the world around us, at a certain point things begin to blur to form the edges of our known world.

The inner edge of our naked-eye reality is where the parts of the parts are about one-thousandth of an inch in diameter. If we assume approximately six feet for the size of a human being, then the naked eye inner edge of our reality is approximately six feet times twelve inches per foot times one-thousand parts per inch—or seventy-two thousand times smaller than a human being.

When we look up into the sky, we see the sun, the moon, the planets, and the stars. The sun and moon look to be the same size and distance above us. The planets and stars are smaller and look as if they are part of a more distant background to the universe. If we did not have our modern technical aids for increasing the power of human sensing, we would assume, like our ancestors, that all the heavenly bodies are located not very far above the tops of the earth's mountains.

The highest mountain in the world is Mount Everest. Its top is about five and one-half miles above sea level, and so the naked eye perceives the distance to the natural objects in the sky to be measured some distance higher—say, approximately eighty-two miles. Eighty-two miles times five thousand two-hundred eighty feet per mile equals 432,960 feet. By dividing this distance by the approximate size of a human (six feet), we calculate that the naked eye outer edge of our reality is about seventy-two thousand times bigger than a human. So the naked eye outer edge of our reality and the naked eye inner edge of our reality both have the same distance relationship to us. This places humanity right in the middle of everything we see.

Over the centuries leading up to the sixteenth century and Copernicus, naked-eye astronomers were watching the sky and recording the movements of the heavenly objects. These calculations mapped out a reality that looked different from that of the Aristotelian model. Copernicus presented new scientific data that indicated the earth and the planets revolve around the sun.

The new sun-centered model changed the presumed center of the mass of everything. But the size of the sun-centered Copernican universe was not any larger than the earth-centered one that it replaced. Copernicus still believed that the stars were attached to the furthest sphere, which represented the outer fixed edge of the universe.

Then early in the seventeenth century, technology took a leap forward. In 1608 Hans Lippershey, a Dutch spectacle maker, invented the spyglass. He discovered that distant things look much closer when looking through a concave and convex lens held in front of each other. He mounted these lenses in a tube. Early spyglasses were used mainly for military purposes, such as observing enemy ships and opposing armies. Glass grinding and polishing technology was already well known, so this new invention was easily copied, and it spread throughout Europe.

Galileo built a much improved and more powerful spyglass. He pointed it toward the heavens, where he saw the heavenly objects in never-before-seen detail. Galileo concluded that the stars were at a tremendous distance, because their sizes did not change, as did the sun, moon, and planets when they were viewed through his telescope. The perception of the seventeenth-century known human reality grew many times larger than before.

Optical telescopes work by collecting and magnifying the visible light coming to the earth from the objects in outer space. Galileo's telescope was what is called a refracting telescope, which uses glass lenses to bend light rays and magnify objects. In 1688 James Gregory, a Scottish astronomer, designed a completely different type of telescope called the reflecting telescope. This design brought light rays to a focus by reflecting them off a curved mirror, producing much better images, because reflecting mirrors could be made much larger than refracting lenses.

Newton built the first working reflecting telescope in the late seventeenth century. He saw the universe in more detail than ever, which helped inspire him to discover the laws of motion and the universal law of gravitation. His formulas were used to calculate the dimensions of the orbits of the known planets. The radius of the earth's orbit was found to be about ninety-three million miles. This is an approximate average, because planetary orbits are elliptical and not perfect circles.

The average diameter of the earth's orbit is two times the radius or one hundred eight-six million miles. This is a large enough shift in the relative position of the earth to pick up the slight movements of some stars in the otherwise motionless map of the starry night sky. In this way the distance to the stars closest to us in our galactic neighborhood could be approximated using the method of stellar parallax, where distance is related to how much shift is seen in plotted positions when comparing maps made from viewing at opposite sides of the orbit. In the Newtonian period the universe was thought to be infinite, but actual calculated outer distances were a mere few trillion (10×10^{12}) miles.

Telescopes continued to be made larger. During the nineteenth century William Parsons, an Irish astronomer, built a six-foot diameter reflector. It was so powerful that much more detail could be seen in the fuzzy patches of light scattered across the sky. It was discovered that these patches of light were actually galaxies—like our own Milky Way— which consist of concentrations of billions of individual stars. The universe was becoming more complex than ever. Scientists began painting a picture indicating our sun is not at the center of our galaxy, and our galaxy is but one of many billions of others that dot the ever-increasing vastness of space.

In the nineteenth century there was a great period of scientific experimentation and discovery. Electricity and electromagnetic radiation were explored and somewhat understood. This understanding was applied to the field of astronomy.

At the beginning of the twentieth century, astronomers noticed the Doppler shifts of distant galaxies. If an object is moving toward an observer, the wavelength is seen as a little shorter. If an object is moving away from an observer, the wavelength is a little longer. Color is related to the wavelength of visible light. A shift toward a longer wavelength causes a shift toward the red end of the visible spectrum. By knowing the degree of color shift, astronomers can determine whether galaxies are moving toward us or away from us, along with how fast they are moving.

In 1929 Edwin Hubble determined that the light coming from most galaxies is shifted toward the red end of the spectrum. The more distant galaxies had more increase in the red shift, and the farther away the galaxy was, the faster it moved. So scientists began to believe that the universe is expanding (accelerating outward) uniformly. This uniform relationship between velocity of expansion and distance from the earth is known as Hubble's law. (This is the genesis of the Big Bang theory of how the universe magically came into existence. Scientists have taken this measurement of light and interpreted it to mean that everything began in a primal "big bang" explosion.)

Light rays are just one part of the electromagnetic spectrum. Stars not only give off visible light; they also give off radio waves, microwaves, infrared light, ultraviolet light, x-rays, and gamma rays. Twentieth-century scientists invented telescopes that detected all of these forms of electromagnetic waves. In 1965 American astrophysicists Arno Penzias and Robert Wilson discovered a constant low temperature radiation coming from all directions in space. (This measurement of cosmic background radiation is believed by scientists to be consistent with the radiation that would theoretically be left over from the big bang explosion.)

Quasars were discovered in the 1950s through the use of radio telescopes. They are believed to be the energetic nucleus of distant galaxies. The spectral lines of quasars show very large red shifts, which indicate these objects are traveling away from the earth at high speeds (up to eighty percent of the speed of light). This also means that quasars are among the most distant of the objects in macro reality. Astronomers using the two-hundred-inch reflector at Palomar Observatory discovered a quasar twelve billion light-years distant in 1991.

While astronomers were expanding the outer dimensions of our reality, other scientists were expanding the inner dimensions. During Galileo's century, a Dutch microscope maker by the name of Antonie van Leeuwenhoek used his optical microscopes to discover and study bacteria. Leeuwenhoek's microscopes could magnify things to three hundred times their actual size. He is considered the founder of microbiology.

Optical microscopes use visible light to create a magnified image of an object. Simple convex lenses can magnify things up to fifteen times their actual size. Compound microscopes use an objective lens and an ocular lens mounted at opposite ends of a tube. The two-lens design can magnify up to two thousand times. The French biologist Louis Pasteur later used a microscope to show that microbes do not arise from nonliving matter as people before him had believed.

John Dalton, a British schoolmaster and chemist, is considered the founder of modern atomic theory. He showed how atoms link together in definite proportions. Later investigations showed that the smallest unit of a chemical substance such as water is a molecule. Each molecule of water consists of two atoms of hydrogen and one atom of oxygen (H_2O) joined by an electrical force called a chemical bond. Hydrogen is the lightest of all atoms. It has a diameter of 1×10^{-10} meters and weighs 1.7×10^{-24} grams. An atom is so small that a single drop of water contains more than one billion trillion (1×10^{21}) atoms.

Before the twentieth century scientists studied the properties of bulk macroscopic matter. The field of particle physics came from the study of smaller and smaller pieces of matter. Around the turn of the twentieth century, scientists directed their attention to trying to figure out how molecules and atoms work. Molecules and atoms have diameters of about 1×10^{-10} meters.

Ernest Rutherford, a British physicist, found that Dalton's atom is divisible. His study of radiation led to his formulation of a theory of atomic structure. In 1919 he discovered positively charged particles in the nucleus of atoms, called protons. His theory described the atom as a dense nucleus of positively charged protons with negatively charged electrons circulating in orbits. Then in 1932 Sir James Chadwick, another British physicist, discovered another type of particle in the nucleus called the neutron. It was electrically neutral.

The atom was found to consist mostly of space. At the center of this space is an infinitesimally small core called the nucleus. The charges carried by all electrons equal the same amount of electricity that resides in the nucleus, so the normal electrical state of the atom is neutral. By the 1930s scientists began to investigate the structure of the atom's nucleus. The size of the nucleus is about 1×10^{-15} meters. The protons and neutrons are held together by extremely powerful nuclear forces. This work led to the development of nuclear bombs and nuclear power generators.

The magnifying power of an optical microscope is limited, because the details of objects cannot be seen if they are smaller than the wavelengths of visible light. The scanning interferometric apertureless microscope was developed to overcome this limitation. It uses a silicon probe one billionth (1×10^{-09}) of a meter wide that vibrates two hundred thousand times per second and scatters a portion of the light passing through an observed sample.

The scattered light is then recombined with non-scattered light to produce an interference pattern that reveals minute details of the sample. Objects can be resolved that are six thousand five hundred times smaller than conventional light microscopes.

An electron microscope uses an electron gun that emits electrons, which then strike an object to illuminate it. Electrons can resolve much smaller detail, because they have a much smaller wavelength than light. The smallest wavelength of light is about forty millionths (4×10^{-05}) of a meter. The wavelength of electrons used in electron microscopes is about fifty trillionths (5×10^{-11}) of a meter.

Scanning electron microscopes can magnify objects one hundred thousand (1×10^{5}) times or more. They can map detailed three-dimensional images of the surface of objects. A scanning probe microscope has a probe with a point as narrow as a single atom. It can scan an object and map out a three-dimensional image of the atoms or molecules on its surface. Scanning transmission electron microscopes can resolve single atoms.

In order to explore inside the atom, scientists have invented a device called a particle accelerator. It is used to accelerate charged elementary particles to high energies. The particles cannot be seen, but their high-energy tracks can be detected. Each different particle has a unique signature track. Particle accelerators have a source of elementary particles, a tube with a vacuum pump (so the particles can travel without hitting air molecules), and a means of speeding up the particles. Particles are intentionally collided with other particles to break matter down to even smaller parts.

In 1963 two researchers, American physicists Murray Gell-Mann and George Zweig, proposed that protons and neutrons are divisible. They found evidence of yet smaller particles they called quarks. It is now theorized that there are six different quarks, three of which combine differently to become either a proton or a neutron. Today's advancing particle detection technology is now allowing researchers to theorize that there are even smaller particles inside the quarks. These sub-quarks are many thousands of times smaller than quarks.

Particle accelerators produce elementary particles that have diameters of between 1×10^{-15} to 1×10^{-18} meters. More than two hundred signatures representing different bits of matter have been revealed, most of which exist for much less than one hundred-millionth of a second.

Scientists continue to push the outer edge of our physical reality and the inner edge of our physical reality. Quasars are currently at the outer edge at twelve billion light years distance. This is an outer radius of 7×10^{22} miles, meaning that the outer edge of our reality is currently about 1×10^{26} times larger than we are.

Sub-quark particles are at the current inner edge, which means that the inner edge of our reality is currently about 1×10^{26} times smaller than we are. So we are still right in the middle of our physical universe.

There are no limits to numbers, but the only numbers that actually do exist are the ones that people actually create. The same is true for distance and space. There is no stopping point in outer space and no stopping point in inner space. Unlimited distance and space are possible, but the only distances and space that actually exist are that which we contemplate and measure.

Copernicus and Galileo started a revolution that has produced inventions that have dramatically increased the power of human sensing. It has been like turning up the zoom in a computer simulation, so we can see more details.

Even after centuries of scientific exploration and discovery, however, neither Galileo nor any subsequent scientist has removed humans from the center of the universe or changed our role in the universal process. The only thing that has changed is that modern science now gives us a much more detailed and complex reality.

Time

Science's systematic assignment of dimensions to objects in space has helped cause us to believe in independent, freestanding volumetric space. This dimensioning only compares the relative sizes of the objects within our interacting reality, however. For example, a participant in a virtual world could measure an object and calculate its volume, but the object would not exist by itself in free space. It requires a computer program and an observer outside of the virtual world in order to exist.

As in a virtual world, there is no evidence that the objects in our real world exist in independent, freestanding volumetric space. Likewise, science's systematic measurements of the relative movements of objects have allowed the assignment of units of time. This has caused us to falsely believe that time is also something that exists as an independent quantity, but units of time only tell us with accuracy dependent on the prevailing technology how much some things change relative to other things. As in a virtual world, there is no evidence in our real world of freestanding time.

The technological advancements of the twentieth century made it possible for people to live in a human-shaped reality. Many of us live in air-conditioned homes and watch television programs. We step into our attached garages and drive our air-conditioned automobiles to our air-conditioned workplaces. Most of us generally have little contact with the natural world.

Within my grandfather's lifetime, humanity has gone from a world filled with an everyday struggle to survive in nature to today's reality of comfortable lifestyles insulated from the natural wonders and dangers of the world. This modern scientific reality reinforces the false perception that space and time are separate from us.

One of my fondest memories of my grandfather was listening to him tell about sailing to America on a schooner in the 1800s. It made me curious about how the sailors of past centuries could find their way from Europe to America across such a vast, open ocean. They spent weeks and months with no method of communication and nothing but water in every direction.

The magnetic compass had already long been invented, and it always pointed to magnetic north, so sailors knew in which general direction they were going. But they needed more information in order to know how far they had traveled and how far the wind had blown them off course. They were often lost and shipwrecked in uncharted waters. Great Britain and other seafaring countries desperately needed a solution.

Knowledge of the correct time was the key to determining location. We humans have divided the day into twenty-four increments called hours, and we have divided the 360 degrees of the earth's map into north–south increments called longitudinal lines. If it is 11 a.m. in London and noon at sea, then the ship has traveled one twenty-fourth the circumference of the earth or 15 degrees of longitude. By knowing the time back at home port when the sun is directly overhead at sea, sailors could chart their location accurately on a map. Eventually clocks were invented and perfected that could keep accurate time despite the pitching and rolling of a ship and the corrosion of salt air.

Our concept of time comes with knowing our position relative to the objects that surround us. One year is one earth orbit of the sun or 365.25 days. One day is one revolution of the earth. Time is a relationship between the movements of things.

We humans have done some refining. A clock is a manmade machine that is designed with indicators that keep pace with natural movements. We arbitrarily divide the day into twenty-four hours, the hour into 60 minutes, the minute into 60 seconds, and so on. These smaller increments or units of time give us the ability to keep track of and coordinate shorter interactions while still referencing all motion to the earth's orbit. Clocks are calibrated to coincide with our moving solar system. Time is an integral part of a moving or changing process.

Space and time exist when things interact with things, but these quantities do not exist separate from the process. If everything would suddenly stop moving, time would not exist. For example, vinyl records, magnetic tapes, and CDs have information embedded in them, but time is not inherently associated with the information. When the information comes to life on a player (humans interact with the information), then time is created. Another example is a video or movie (motion picture). When a person watches a movie, he or she processes it as real motion in real time. We immerse ourselves into an imaginary space and time.

As I get older I can personally see how time is a function of my interaction with reality and not something that exists separate from me. When I first learned about George Washington and Ben Franklin, the founding of the United States was twenty times older than me. The

Revolutionary War seemed like ancient history. But, today this same time span is only three of my lifetimes, so now it does not seem very far in the past at all. It seems more like modern history. Time is something that is subject to human interpretation.

Time does not stand alone as a fixed quantity. Understanding that time exists only when the mind is interacting with the world becomes very important when we think of the history of the universe and how humanity fits into it. Our physical reality does not exist in space and time without us.

Scientific Theory of God: Proof that God Exists ~ John Michael Thompson

CHAPTER EIGHT

Creation

Scientists claim the world exists because of evolution and not creation. What scientists don't realize is that evolution is a necessary part of creation.

It has always been very difficult for me to swallow the modern scientific claim that the world I am experiencing is the result of an atom-sized explosion and a subsequent period of fourteen or fifteen billion years of evolutionary change. Scientists claim our entire universe along with its complex organisms arose out of nothing. They make this claim without even knowing what space, time, and matter are in the first place. Really!

It seems to me that the universe is a process, and like all processes it is constantly changing. The natural world is constantly being pushed and pulled, causing everything to change into something else. Mutating and evolving would be natural whether or not the universe was created by God, but it is a scientific stretch—to say the least—to measure, extrapolate, and interpret today's snapshot of a changing process as proof that it all started with a big bang. It is like saying a jet plane accelerating west over California must have started out in New York City at a certain time.

But the situation is even more convoluted. It turns out that later evidence does not match the original big bang theory. Again it's like Ptolemy's epicycles: modern scientists have had to cook the books by inserting what they call inflation (extra-temporary acceleration) in order to make the model seem to work. Scientists can measure what is going on now, but they really do not know the path that got us here.

The design of virtual worlds gives us insight into our own real-world creation. A virtual world is a mathematical creation operating in present time. Like our real world, it has all the supporting details necessary to give it a past history, which includes things like a planet, water, minerals, plants, and animals. These things must pre-exist before the virtual participants are immersed within the reality. Scientists in an active virtual world could take measurements and claim it all started at some point in the distant past, but this would only be a perception. They would not be aware of the nonphysical, not-in-space-and-time creation process.

We know from designing virtual realities that a creation is an idea turned into reality. First, the idea is laid out in a blueprint or program. After the program is completed, the participants are immersed, and the reality is acted out in four-dimensional space-time. The whole design necessarily has a seamless physical connection, so that everything, from the participants' time perspective, flows from the past to the present and on into the future.

We can't presume to understand the thoughts of our Creator, but we are capable of studying and figuring out how the reality he created—and we live in—works. When our universe was created, it must have been similar to the way we human designers create our virtual realities, but of course ours are on a vastly smaller and vastly less sophisticated scale. The Creator of our reality would have had to make all living and nonliving things interactively compatible and would have had to provide a ready environment to make it possible for humanity to survive.

Our early ancestors believed that the earth, the heavens, the plants, and the animals were created first, and then humans were placed here to interact for better or worse. The modern world-view is in direct conflict with this ancient world-view, so now it is hard for us to believe in biblical creation. But when we analyze the universe as an unlimited human reality instead of a freestanding reality, then we can see that the historical evidence actually agrees more closely with the ancient creation story.

Interpretation of the Old Testament indicates that creation took place in one week approximately six thousand years ago. During the first five days humans were provided the resources necessary to survive and prosper before immersing them into the activity on the sixth day. The story claims God rested on the seventh day. Now, it seems that this biblical account wasn't too different from what we might expect in a human interactive reality, except for the time frame. Our ancestors had no way of understanding the nonphysical aspect of the universe, so the timeline of creation was interpreted based on very limited technical knowledge.

Much preparation is required before a reality program is ready for its participants to be installed at the controls. This is true for all interactive realities, including the one that we live in, but no universe is an active four-dimensional physical world until the participants start the interaction.

We see movies and television programs that show stone-age people being chased by dinosaurs. This gives us a false impression that our human ancestors and the dinosaurs lived side by side at the dawn of humanity. The geological record and the fact that dinosaurs and other prehistoric animals existed make us believe that the earth is much older than six thousand years. The dinosaurs lived and then disappeared many millions of years before we humans arrived on the scene. Dinosaur fossils have been found spread over the world's continents, covered by tens of millions of years of shifting landmass, silt, and blowing sand.

People ask the question, "If the universe was created for humanity, then why did the dinosaurs live and die before the arrival of humans?" The answer is that humanity needs the heavens, the earth, the minerals, the plants, and the animals all in the right conditions in order to have the opportunity to survive and advance.

The pre-human world was in a stage of nonphysical design just like a human programmer would design a computer reality. Space and time did not exist in the pre-human universe, but now modern scientists analyze from the inside out and falsely interpret the pre-human period as physically existing without humans and spanning billions of human years.

Modern humans have gradually pieced together an apparent timeline of the history of our world and its inhabitants. An early method for determining the age of the earth was to count the generations in the Bible. This was first done in the seventeenth century by Archbishop James Ussher, and it is how the six-thousand-year age of the world was calculated. In the eighteenth century, the French scientist George-Louis Leclerc determined an age of seventy-five thousand years based on how fast it takes iron to cool down. In the nineteenth century, geologists calculated the time it would take minerals to wash off the land into the sea and accumulate to the present salt content. They also calculated how long it would take for layers of sediment to accumulate. These and other studies of the earth's erosion produced claims that the earth is many millions of years old.

Charles Darwin argued that it must have taken hundreds of millions of years for the slow process of evolution to result in our modern level of sophistication. In the twentieth century, technology advanced to where the ages of minerals and rocks could be measured by radiometric dating. Some rocks were determined to be over two billion years old. Paleontologists have found thousands of different animal fossils. Some of these fossils are determined to be hundreds of millions of years old. Most of the animals represented are extinct. The oldest modern human remains are not much more than one hundred thousand years old.

This physical evidence gives us the perception that the earth was around long before its human inhabitants. Because of this evidence, most of us now believe the universe is something that existed and continues to exist independently of living things and is evolving on its own due to its own momentum. We humans have been downgraded to relatively powerless beings. This false belief causes many people to question the validity of their religious world-view. Even our modern churches are changing their doctrines in order to explain the human role in the modern nonhuman world-view.

It is indisputable that the universe is a physical process that is evolving and changing over time, but contrary to popular belief evolution does not mean we live in a mindless material world. Evolutionary change is just what you would expect in a human cosmos, but we are not helpless byproducts of the evolutionary process. We live in a changing program designed so that free will interaction can take place—or else we would not have the power to influence the world around us.

Just as a virtual reality is a mathematical creation, our actual reality is a mathematical creation. We know this to be true because scientists can describe the natural world in mathematical terms. Our universe is an unbounded, mathematically describable physical environment that is fully compatible with all of its living participants. We participants are immersed into the reality, so that our minds can sense, interpret, and perceive the universe in three-dimensional space, time, and matter. There are rules embedded in the program so that there is order and everything can interact in seamless motion. The Creator incorporated the physical forces into nature so that everything is physically interconnected; therefore the whole process can be pushed and pulled and shaped as time flows from past to present to future.

Our free-will interaction within our real reality can be better understood by examining computer games. A computer game is designed with a specific environment where the interaction takes place. The program is designed to play out or evolve over time according to a programmed cause-and-effect sequence of events, which can only be altered when the human players use their free will to control their virtual bodies and influence the course of action. Each free-will change puts the game on a new course; there are unlimited possible futures or outcomes of the game. But the human part of the computer game is not a physical part of the computer simulation. The players have a computer (virtual) body, but they control it from outside of the computer reality, the same way our nonphysical soul controls our physical body from outside of our real reality.

All participants' bodies are designed and constructed with the same compatible features so they can sense, interact, and communicate with each other and their surroundings. The Creator designed our world so that everything operates within the same electromagnetic ranges, so all living organisms can interact within the system. Darwin's theory of evolution confirms this design by presenting the physical evidence that all living things are biologically related and that life has evolved from a single design.

We know how processes are created, so we should not think that God just waved a magic wand. God would have had to do preliminary, step-by-step programming to arrive at the environmental conditions necessary to support living participants. Our planet is located the perfect distance from the sun, so that we are exposed to the perfect temperature range. We live on a perfectly sized planet with the perfect amount of gravity. The heat energy stored within the earth allows it to constantly renew itself. Volcanic actions and other natural phenomena have caused the earth to separate out its minerals into natural deposits, so that we humans can use our imaginations to shape the natural elements into the wonderful inventions we enjoy today.

The amount of water on the earth is in just the right proportion, so that we have the proper amount of evaporation and rainfall, which helps sustain a large and diverse plant and animal population. The sun provides the energy for plants to grow. It has been necessary for plants to live and decay for many millions of years in order for large and concentrated fossil fuel energy supplies to accumulate. Our modern Earth is rich in the wood, coal, gas, and oil without which today's advanced human civilization would not be possible.

Much physical evidence has been accumulated and a scientific picture of history has emerged. From our human perspective as participants, the earth appears to be about 4.6 billion years old. The oldest rocks that have been found are about four billion years old. So the first six hundred million years of the Earth's existence were very hot and violent. The Precambrian Period spanned from the beginning of geological history four billion years ago to the Cambrian Period, which began about five hundred seventy million years ago. The Cambrian Period marked the beginning of multiple-celled life forms.

The continents began to form during the Precambrian Period by a process called plate tectonics. The earth's crust is lighter and cooler than its interior, which is hot and semi-liquid. The surface crust moves under the power of gravity and heat convection. The continents float and slowly drift on the earth's surface and sometimes collide, forming a range of geological formations including mountain ranges. It is theorized that the continents broke up and re-formed several times during the latter part of the Precambrian Period. Minerals essential to modern human survival such as lead, gold, and uranium were formed during this period.

The atmosphere was formed from the gasses escaping from the hot interior of the earth. This primal atmosphere consisted of carbon dioxide and water. Gravity is the force that holds the atmosphere above the surface of the earth. A smaller planet's gravity is not strong enough to keep its gases from escaping into outer space. When the earth was hot, its water was in the form of vapor as part of the atmosphere. The oceans were formed as the earth cooled and the water vapor condensed on the earth's surface.

It is theorized that around four billion years ago the first life forms consisting of primitive bacteria originated in the hot spots at the bottom of the ocean. In theory, heat, water, carbon dioxide, and methane were at the perfect set of conditions for a chemical reaction. According to evolutionary scientists, all life on Earth today is descended from this original spontaneous chemical reaction. This evidence does not disagree with the human model, because it also describes all life originating from a first single design.

The Precambrian Period, which began about 2.5 billion years ago, is divided into the early Archean Eon and the latter Proterozoic Eon. During the Archean Eon cells evolved that could produce their own food through the process of photosynthesis. Photosynthesis is where the energy of light is used to convert carbon dioxide and water into the simple sugar glucose. Photosynthesis supplies the energy for almost all organisms. Most organisms cannot exist without oxygen, which is an essential byproduct of photosynthesis.

The development of the nucleus enclosed in a membrane is believed to have happened during the Proterozoic Eon. Also during this period, life forms developed specialized organs for respiration, food storage, and sexual reproduction. This created genetic diversity and gave an organism the ability to survive environmental change. The oxygen levels in the atmosphere and the oceans were increasing, which allowed multiple-celled organisms to evolve.

From seven hundred to five hundred seventy million years ago the blueprints for modern animals were created during an explosion of evolutionary diversification. First on the scene were the jellyfish, and then various worm types evolved. Skeletons developed independently in various types of animals.

The Phanerozoic Eon began with the Cambrian period and continues through our modern times. The Phanerozoic Eon is divided into the Paleozoic Era, the Mesozoic Era, and the Cenozoic Era.

The Paleozoic era covered the period five hundred seventy to three hundred thirty million years ago. Fish, shellfish, fern forests, insects, land plants, reptiles, and amphibians evolved during this era. Large plant populations were critical, because advanced land animal populations could not survive without them. These plants expanded from the swamps and developed into large green zones. The first creatures to walk on land were reptiles. Over a long period of time, they crawled out of the ocean and adapted to the environment of the land.

The Mesozoic Era covered from three hundred thirty million to one hundred million years ago. Reptiles comparable to the crocodile evolved into dinosaurs during this era. Also small mammals, birds, and flowering plants emerged. Dinosaurs were the dominant animals for about one hundred thirty-five million years. Mammals evolved from reptiles about two hundred million years ago and lived in the shadows of the dinosaurs for one hundred million years. The transition from reptile to mammal was very slow, with a gradual development of mammalian features. Mammals developed a warm-blooded lifestyle, fur, and mammary glands, all of which would become great assets.

The shape of the continents and oceans were very different when the dinosaurs ruled the earth. All the land was connected into a massive continent called Pangaea, which was surrounded by a single vast ocean called Panthalassa. The force of energy inside the earth caused Pangaea to slowly break up and form today's continents by the end of the dinosaur period. This separation of a single land mass into several land masses also resulted in the separation of plants and animals. This phenomenon exposed the earth's plants and animals to a much wider variety of environments. Some plant and animal species became extinct, but many new plant and animal species evolved to take their places.

There was a worldwide mass extinction about sixty-five million years ago. All of the dinosaurs were eradicated, but the smaller mammals were able to survive. Scientists theorize that an asteroid or a comet came from outer space and plowed into the earth. This type of event would have thrown debris from the earth up into the atmosphere, which would have blocked out sunlight for many months. This extended lack of sunlight would have killed most of the plants and deprived large animals of their main food source. The large plant eaters would have died of starvation, which in turn would have starved the animals that preyed on them. This mass extinction was a gift to humanity, because the elimination of the dinosaurs created the space and the environmental conditions for our small mammal predecessors to survive and evolve into the most successful form of life form in the universe.

After the dinosaurs were killed off, mammals could no longer be held back. They found themselves with an abundance of opportunity. Since that time mammals have evolved into a vast variety of shapes and sizes. Today there are several thousand species of mammals. Almost all have four limbs and live on the land, but some like the whale have gone back to the sea.

Mammals are warm-blooded, which give them the ability to closely maintain body temperature. This feature has allowed mammals to adapt to a wide range of environmental conditions, and spread to the far corners of the earth. Mammals have developed large brains and a high intelligence compared to other animals. This gives mammals the advantage of a high level of resourcefulness.

There are many similarities between mammal species, which gives evidence that they evolved from a common life form. Almost all mammals have seven vertebrae in their necks, and the arms of humans, the flippers of seals, and the wings of bats all have the same number and arrangement of bones. These are just two examples.

The Cenozoic Era began one hundred million years ago and continues to present times. Human beings, primates, grazing animals, and carnivores evolved during this time. Primitive apes spread over Africa, Europe, and Asia from between seven and twenty million years ago. Scientists have compared the DNA of apes to the DNA of modern humans. The scientific result shows that the evolutionary split of humans from chimpanzees and gorillas happened six to eight million years ago. This split was the precursor to our small-brained human ancestors.

Scientists have discovered many human fossils of different types and ages. This collection of remains shows that human evolution began more than four million years ago in eastern and southern Africa. The evidence suggests that between two and three million years ago there may have been more than two separate species of humans. Stone tools have been found in African sites from around this period. One of these early human species evolved into genus Homo and eventually into modern humans. A species of large-brained humans emerged in Africa about two million years ago, and then later a similar species appeared in Asia. The African species is called Homo ergaster. The Asian species is called Homo erectus. Scientists think that Homo ergaster spread into Asia and evolved into Homo erectus.

Homo ergaster evolved into Homo sapiens between two hundred thousand and three hundred thousand years ago. These earliest examples of Homo sapiens were very good at adapting to the extreme climates of Ice Age Europe. It was during this period that human beings first began to purposefully bury their dead. Stone tools, animal bones, and flowers were sometimes buried in the graves with the bodies. This is evidence that early humans had a belief in an after-life.

According to the fossil record, our big-brained ancestors evolved in Africa and the Middle East between ninety thousand and two hundred thousand years ago. The human brain tripled in size over the time of this human development. The continued development of activities like social interrelationships, tool making, and tool use was the probable cause of this increase in brain size. Our big-brained human ancestors developed speech and language, which has subsequently had a profound impact on human interaction. Our ancestors were able to adapt to a wide range of environmental conditions, which enabled them to spread around the world.

Humans could not have survived and evolved without animals. Hunting animals has played a critical role in supplying food and other materials necessary for survival. Approximately fourteen thousand years ago humans began to manage the way animals live and breed. The dog was probably the first animal to be domesticated and was probably developed from the wolf. People followed and hunted herds and then learned to control them. Controlled breeding produced different breeds for different human requirements. Horses were bred for work and transportation. Cattle were bred for meat, milk, and hides. Sheep were raised for food and wool.

Approximately ten thousand years ago people discovered how to domesticate plants. Farming was one of the most important developments in all of human history. The agricultural revolution was a world-changing event that put humanity on the path toward civilization and today's modern world.

We humans have been designed and developed by God to rule the earth and the universe. The age of the dinosaurs as well as all pre-human evolution played a vital role in our evolutionary development. The time before humans stocked the world with large amounts of diverse plants, animals, and natural resources. The history of the earth is not a backward-in-time extrapolation. Evolution is a fundamental part of the universe's design and operation. It is an integral part of God's grand design. This is not hard to understand, because a human computer programmer creating a virtual computer world would go through a very similar not-in-space-and-time evolutionary design process in preparation for the arrival of inhabitants.

The biology of the human life form is rooted in lower forms of animals. We can look into the past to when the chimpanzee's ancestors and our pre-human ancestors were the same. Since then we have taken a different path. The fact that we evolved along with all life forms is a necessary part of God's physical design to enable humanity to be an interactive player in the universe process. But this does not diminish our central role in the universe, because the human soul is separate from its physical form. The soul was not embedded until the human life form was highly evolved. Only then did our interaction begin to transform the universe program into the four-dimensional space-time reality in which we live.

Despite scientists' claims to the contrary, evolution does not disprove God. The opposite is true. A common biological beginning establishes the foundation for every living and non-living thing to physically exist and interact seamlessly within God's program. We humans were given the perfect environment with all the necessities. Our world is certainly too perfect for random chance evolution. Everything was designed and molded so that we humans can survive and impose our free will on the entire cosmos.

CHAPTER NINE

The Human Universe Model

Modern scientists claim the universe is a totally independent material system with no direct connection to human beings. This means the universe would exist whether or not human beings exist. This means it would be fixed in space and time with fixed boundaries big and small, so it would have limits. This physical reality would be totally disconnected from humanity and its far reaches would be unknown and mysterious to our human intellectual capabilities. This disconnected universe would overwhelm us.

In this type of universe we humans would be evolutionary accidents of nature, and there would be no specific purpose for human life. In such a world, we humans would be insignificant animals temporarily residing on a small planet lost in space and time. This would mean we come into existence from nothing and then fade away to nothing. This would mean there is no more to the human journey than what we experience here on Earth, so our lives would be meaningless. This is today's scientific world-view, and many people believe it, but it is wrong.

If Isaac Newton were a virtual scientist analyzing the physical workings within an interactive virtual world, he would discover universal mathematical equations of motion and gravity. These equations would vary depending on how the reality was programmed. And just as he did in our real world, there too he would wrongly conclude it is freestanding and self-powered, because he would not be able to sense and measure the nonphysical not-in-space-and-time part of the virtual reality.

It is great that we think scientifically, so we can mold the elements of nature into the inventions that improve our standard of living, but we should not at the same time disconnect ourselves from the reality we live in. We can see that we are connected to our surroundings. It is not hard to look around and understand that everybody and everything is connected in a continuous interactive process. Science itself has shown that every physical thing—including the human life form—is made from the same elements of nature (neutrons, protons, and electrons). Everything and everyone is all tied together within the same physical system.

A universe connected to human thought is not a new or radical idea. The best philosophers and scientists in history have been engaged in the debate, but it has been a difficult mystery even for these great thinkers—but they did not have the advantage of today's computer technology. Some past scientists speculated that objects are freestanding in a strictly objective universe (this turned out to be the modern model), and some speculated that objects exist only in the mind as a strictly ideal universe. As it has turned out, neither is right.

Fortunately, with the advent of today's virtual technology, it is now possible not only for scientists but for all of us to see that the mind and soul do have the power to be directly connected to the physical object world they interact with. Our solid world is generated in our mind, but it originates in a nonphysical (not in space and time) realm that is beyond our sensory apparatus.

The interaction between the human mind and the object world is a process that works in a designed way. The fact that our minds transform nonphysical information into solid worlds during virtual simulations means that the solid objects in our real world also originate from the nonphysical realm. It is the same process. We live in a technologically advanced time when we can all experience firsthand and understand the soul's direct connection to the world in which it finds itself. We humans are becoming the technical masters of the universe. Computer simulations have advanced to where complex human activities can be modeled.

For example astronauts can be trained to pilot spacecraft before going into space. More recent improvements in computer power, programming, and sensory technology have allowed for the development of a more advanced interactive system called virtual reality. This system allows a user to disconnect from the sensations of the real universe as he or she is immersed in the sights, sounds, and feelings of a human-created universe. The human participant with a virtual body moves around within the three-dimensional virtual space and interacts with the virtual environment as if it were made of solid objects.

At the beginning of the twenty-first century we are rapidly approaching the point where we will be able to create actual life-like and seemingly solid worlds. For example, a person will be able to vacation in exotic faraway lands without ever leaving home. We will not be able to tell the difference. We can experience firsthand what in the past was the stuff of science fiction and see that the soul really can convert a nonphysical information universe into a solid world that it lives within.

Contrary to what scientists claim, scientific discovery actually shows that our universe is not fixed and limited, because there is no largest outer edge or smallest inner particle. There are no edges that limit our reality. Like a virtual reality generated by a human being, our real reality is also unlimited, which means it is also generated by human beings. Newton's equations contain the proof that our physical universe is made from space, and space is a manifestation of the mind and soul. Therefore the scientific evidence shows that the physical world we live in is directly connected to our minds, which are unlimited, and so the human universe is unlimited. It is shaped and expanded by humanity. The scientific evidence proves that the physical universe comes from us, so we are the focus of everything.

Our unlimited universe is an interactive reality where everything in it, including our human bodies, is interconnected to form a dynamic, continually changing reality. Our solid world is experienced as we interact with the universe program, so we are each always at the center. Our unlimited universe grows larger with the expansion of human technical capabilities. Our scientists continue to find more space and more objects not because of the existence of infinite space with an infinite number of objects, but because God designed our interactive universe with endless possibilities.

All around each of us there are physical processes at work. Things are continually interacting with things in the process of changing. We human beings have found ourselves living at the center of the universe process. We are looking from the inside out. Our reality consists of the things and places we are able to see or otherwise experience with our five main human senses. Without these senses, we would be aware of nothing. We would not know we exist.

Our material world includes all of the things that all humans have discovered, but each of us individual humans experiences it through our own unique window. The human cosmos is the total of all individual human universes, but the total human universe is much bigger than any one human can know about, because the total of human knowledge is much more than any one single person can accumulate. This is a reason why we get the false impression that the universe is disconnected and infinite.

Like the Internet, where millions of computers are connected together to form the total Internet universe, the total is much more than the information on any single computer. We imagine that there is vastly more that exists beyond our known human world, but there is not. The cosmos is no bigger or smaller than the size and detail of all the accumulated knowledge from all the humans that have ever lived.

The total known cosmos is the accumulation of all the knowledge contributed by humans throughout human history, but each human knows a different object world created only from the amount of information he or she has accumulated. Therefore a fixed freestanding cosmos with a fixed center does not exist. What we see or otherwise sense through our window is all we know or can ever know. All of humanity pushes and pulls the process, but each person is in the center of and has the power to control his or her own physical universe.

We are each one window of billions in the universe, and we each assume that every other human being interacts within the universal process in this same way. An individual human being can be pushed and pulled by his or her surroundings, or an individual human being can push and pull his or her surroundings. We humans are continually processing our universe and transforming it into a larger and more complex physical reality.

A way to visualize and understand how our reality grows is to imagine that you are a participant in a virtual world. You are in a room with other participants. Nothing in the reality exists as solid three-dimensional objects except the things you can sense: your virtual body, the interior of the room, and the other people and objects in it. There are several doors that lead out of the room. As a free-will participant, you can choose any one of the doors, but solid objects do not exist behind the doors until you open one, expose your mind to the program, interact with it, and expand the space of your reality.

Every individual is unique. When we look around, we each see a universe full of objects. We see other people, buildings, trees, the sky, the sun, the moon, the stars, and millions of other things. We read books, watch television, and listen to other people. We see different things from different perspectives and therefore interpret differently. Each of us has a picture of the universe that was formed from all that has entered our mind. We each live in a different universe, so we are each at the center of our own physical world, which no one else can see or understand. How much detail we see and experience determines the size and complexity of each of our individual realities.

Modern scientists are wrong to think the cosmos starts from the smallest fundamental particle and builds up to the largest structural thing. Everything starts with us. We are the information processors. We create our reality from the inside out as we explore, discover, invent, and build the world we want to live in. Hopefully, we will know God, talk to God, and redeem ourselves.

The Forces of Nature

"Let no one enter here who is ignorant of mathematics"

~ Inscription over the door of Plato's academy

Scientific discovery works just as well for the human interactive model as it does for the modern scientific freestanding model. Classical physics, the theory of relativity, and quantum mechanics as well as all other proven scientific relationships in nature are equally valid for both models, because the difference is not with how things act but with how things exist. When scientists measure the motions and forces between interacting objects, the information does not tell whether the universe is freestanding or not. This is one reason scientists are confused. The action formulas work, but they can't find the edges, they don't know what matter is, and they can't explain what gravity, electricity, or the nuclear forces are or how these forces of nature connect into a unified process. Scientists wrongly assume that if the formulas work, then the model must be correct. The fact is the modern scientific freestanding model is wrong and must be discarded.

The universe is not freestanding. We must change science to the human interactive model, which does solve the mysteries of the universe. Newton's equations confirm that objects are made of space and time, so the physical manifestation of the things in our real world is taking place in the mind. The whole physical cosmos is connected to the mind, so the whole physical cosmos can be defined in terms of space and time. This chapter will define the unified force equation in terms of space and time. Existing scientific equations are special cases of this new unified equation.

Let's start with a review of Chapter Four. From experience we know that it takes a lot more force to move a heavy thing than to move a light thing. For example we can throw a baseball a lot farther than we can throw a bowling ball, because all things inherently have something associated with them called inertia, which is defined as a thing's reluctance to change its position or velocity. Inertia is also a measure of the gravitational attraction that an object exerts on another object. There is a known connection between space and gravity.

Newton's equation of motion shows that an object has more mass than another object if it takes more force to accelerate it through space than the other object. We also know that an object in a gravitational field is more massive (weighs more) than another object if it has more force applied to it by gravity than the other object. So if mass shows up when an object is being accelerated through space, then the same phenomenon must be occurring when mass shows up in a gravitational field. Therefore a gravitational field and accelerated space must be the same thing. Since it has been shown that every object has gravity proportional to its amount of mass, space is accelerating into all objects. In the case of Earth, space is accelerating downward into the particles that form the planet, which causes a high flow at the surface.

Because of its mysterious previous existence, mass has been given an arbitrary name called the kilogram. It is defined as force-time squared divided by distance. In other words mass is related to force, time, and distance. When we rearrange Newton's three-hundred-year-old equations and solve for mass, we easily find that mass equals distance cubed divided by time squared. In other words, a material reality is made up of accelerated space.

The constant G always shows up when calculating gravitational forces, but its value was not at first known. Gravity is very weak in the objects of our everyday environment, so it is very difficult to measure. The gravitational force between two humans standing at one-meter distance from each other is about eighty-five billionths (85×10^{-9}) of a pound, a very insignificant force in our daily lives. But in 1798 English chemist and physicist Henry Cavendish measured G with a very sensitive experiment. He was able to measure gravity, because he was able to remove the effects of friction, air movements, and other forces from the environment of the experiment. The value he found was 6.754×10^{-11} newton x meter^2/kilogram^2, close to the currently accepted value of 6.670×10^{-11} newton x meter^2/kilogram^2.

We need to understand the units of measure that are used to express the value of the gravitational constant G, so we can get an understanding of what kind of quantity it is. The metric system is normally used in scientific expressions. The metric units for the value of G are newton x meter^2/kilogram^2. The meter represents a unit of distance, the kilogram represents a unit of mass, and the newton represents a unit of force. Therefore in unit terms,

G = force x distance^2/mass^2

The definition of velocity is distance per time.

$v = d/t$

The definition of acceleration is velocity per time or distance per time^2.

$a = v/t = (d/t)/t = d/t^2$

We know that force = mass x acceleration. Therefore, force = mass x distance /time^2 When we substitute these units of force into the equation for G, we get:

$G = $ *(mass x distance / time^2) x distance^2 / mass^2 = distance^3 / time^2 / mass.*

$G = $ *distance^3/time^2 per unit of mass*

Newton's gravitational constant G is a measure of volumetric space accelerating per unit of mass.

We know that our minds interact with incoming information and generate a four-dimensional solid world. This gives us insight into the space-time-object process. Virtual reality shows that space is created in the mind, and solid objects are formed within the space. So by analyzing the physical world using space as the only ingredient, we can define matter and solve the scientific mysteries of the universe.

Let's investigate the nature of space. Space flows according to the standard fluid flow formula:

$Q = Av$

Where Q is the volumetric flow, A is the area of flow, and v is the velocity of the stream at a particular cross-sectional area. The volumetric flow is constant and the area of flow is variable, so there is a change in velocity (acceleration) that is proportional to the change in area.

This rule of fluid flow is related to Newton's universal law of gravity. As space flows downward into the earth, the flowing stream speeds up (accelerates) as the cross-sectional flow area gets smaller. The volume of space surrounding the earth could be considered a funnel with unlimited height, with the earth being at the bottom of the funnel. Space flows down toward the earth. The area of the top is the surface area of a sphere surrounding the earth. The area at a given radius (r) from the center of the earth would be the surface area of a sphere with radius (r). The acceleration of volumetric space flowing down is proportional to the change in the surface area of the sphere. The surface area A of a sphere is mathematically expressed as

$$A = 4\pi r^2$$

So the acceleration of space flowing onto the earth is inversely proportional to the square of the distance from the earth. This is exactly as expressed in Newton's equation for universal gravitational force, and it intuitively makes sense that space is flowing down into the earth. If it takes a force to accelerate an object through space, then it follows that a

155

force will act on an object when it is exposed to accelerating space.

Calculations using this new theory confirm that the measured gravitational acceleration g at the earth's surface is 9.84 meter/second^2. The earth's surface area A = $4\pi r^2$, or 5.1 x 10^{14} meter^2. So the total volumetric space acceleration at the earth's surface is gA, which is 5.018 x 10^{15} meter^3/second^2. By dividing this number by the earth's total mass, we get the volumetric space acceleration per kilogram. (5.018 x 10^{15} meter^3/second^2) / (5.98 x 10^{24} kg) = (8.39 x 10^{-10} meter^3/second^2) per kilogram. This happens to be the true value of the gravitational constant G. The currently accepted measurements and calculations do not take into account that the force of gravity is actually proportional to the surface area of flow, not just the radius from the center of the earth. Newton's universal equation should be expressed as

F = G(true)mm/4πr^2

The currently accepted value of G is mistakenly off by a factor of 4π. When we divide the true value of G by 4π, we get 6.67 x 10^{-11} meter^3/second^2 per kilogram, which is the currently accepted value of G.

All particles (objects) are made of accelerated space. Space flows through macro reality and causes a gravitational attraction and then continues to increase in velocity on its downward flow into micro reality. Space flows through micro reality where atomic and sub-atomic particles are formed. This downward acceleration of space causes the electromagnetic and nuclear forces that glue these particles together. The entire physical universe is made of and held together by the downward acceleration of space.

But large-scale processes do not behave in the same way as small-scale processes. The surface area of a stream changes in proportion to the square of the radius, but the volume of the stream changes in proportion to the cube of the radius. So a small stream will have a much higher surface-to-volume ratio. This same surface area to volume change takes place when volumetric space flows in a continuous stream from macro reality to micro reality.

This means that there are different conditions at different levels of reality that cause nature to act differently. According to Newton's equation, the gravitational forces at the atomic level are insignificant. Powerful electrical forces are responsible for gluing atoms together, and they appear to be a completely different phenomenon.

By returning to the funnel analogy, we can visualize how the forces of the universe are connected within the same physical process. As a product moves down, the volume at the top moves slowly while the volume at the bottom moves much faster. In the case of space flowing into the earth, the surrounding volumetric space moves slowly and results in the gravitational force, but as the volumetric space continues to accelerate down into the atomic world, the velocity becomes much higher and results in the electrical force. And as the volumetric space continues down, the velocity becomes incredibly higher and results in the nuclear forces.

The density of a stream also changes as its environment changes. As a product flows down, the product on top compresses the product at the bottom, so the volumetric flow changes due to density as well as area. The same is true for space. As space flows down into micro reality, the volumetric flow changes due to a change in density. Therefore the acceleration of space changes due to a changing flow channel area and due to a changing volumetric flow rate. The flow rate changes due to the changing density of space, and the flow channel area changes due to the ever-decreasing spherical volume of space.

The basic workings of the universal process are mathematically expressed in the following unified equation:

We know the equation for volumetric flow rate is

$Q = Av$

Solving this equation for v, we get

$v = Q/A$

We know that acceleration (a) is equal to the change in velocity, so

$$a = d(v)/dt = d(Q/A)/dt = m/4\pi r^2 - Qv/2\pi r^3, \text{ where } A$$

$= 4\pi r^2$ and $dQ/dt = mass$ (m). Furthermore, $F = ma = mm/4\pi r^2 - mQv/2\pi r^3$

This is the equation that explains the continuous interactions of our physical reality and unifies the forces of nature. It defines the forces acting in all parts of our reality from the outer reaches of macro reality to the inner reaches of micro reality.

As we can see there are two parts to this universal equation. Gravitational, electromagnetic, and nuclear forces are all derived from it. The first half of the equation is inversely proportional to r^2 and the second half is inversely proportional to r^3. When calculating the force field around large objects, r is large, so r^3 becomes vastly larger than r^2, and the second half of the unified equation becomes insignificantly small and drops out. This explains why gravity is long range and nuclear forces are short range. For macro reality, the unified equation becomes

$$F = mm/4\pi r^2 - 0 = mm/4\pi r^2$$

This is exactly Newton's universal equation for gravitational force. Again, constant G is only necessary to adjust when using specific units.

When calculating the force field around small objects, r is small, so r^3 becomes vastly smaller than r^2, and the first half of the equation becomes insignificantly small and drops out. So for micro reality, the unified equation becomes

$$F = 0 - mQv/2\pi r^3 = -mQv/2\pi r^3$$

When nuclear particles combine to form the nucleus of an atom, the space surrounding the proton-neutron assembly rotates, like water going down a drain. This happens at a particular density in space. The angular acceleration of space around the atomic nucleus generates a particular frequency, which is detected as discrete particles called electrons. When calculating the electrical force field in the atomic world, r is very small. So we use the micro half of the universal equation $F = mQv/2\pi r^3$, but it must be adjusted to incorporate constant density.

$$D = m/V$$

Where D is the density of space, m is the mass of space, and V is the volume of space (a sphere when calculating the volume of an atom).

$$V = (4/3)\pi r^3$$

By applying the formulas for the velocity, area, volume, and density to the universal equation, we get $F = mQv/2\pi r^3 = mQQ/2\pi r^3 A = (m/V)QQ/6\pi r^2 = DQQ/6\pi r^2$

This force is proportional to the inverse square of the distance and is identical to Coulomb's equation for electricity, where $K = D/6\pi$ and $q = Q$

The universal equation can be expressed as the relationship between mass and energy.

$$F = m(Av)v/2\pi r^3 = m4\pi r^2 v^2/2\pi r^3 = 2mv^2/r$$

Energy E equals force times distance.

$$E = Fr$$

When we apply the formula for energy to the universal equation, we get

$$E = (2mv^2/r)r = 2mv^2$$

For maximum energy, we need to substitute v for c, which is the speed of light and maximum velocity.

It should be noted here that for simplification, the unified equation has been presented assuming uniform spherical objects and uniform flow of space. In nature, shapes are imperfect, and space does not flow uniformly. This is why Newton's equation does not always fit and is one of the reasons Einstein needed to develop the general theory of gravity to account for a universe that is more complex than previously thought.

The unified equation for acceleration should be expressed and used more generally as $a = (1/A)dQ/dt + Q(d(1/A)/dt)$.

The area of flow A is formulated to reflect the actual complex shape of the object, which would have a more complex force field.

Our physical reality consists only of space (distance^3) and time (t). All of nature can be expressed as a function of distance and time. We already define length (d), area (d^2), and volume (d^3) as functions of distance; we already define velocity (d/t) and acceleration (d/t^2) as functions of distance and time; and we already define frequency as the inverse of time (1/t). Now by substituting the new unified units of mass (d^3/t^2) for the old arbitrary mysterious units of mass in all existing scientific expressions, a complete scientific space-time reality is definable.

Space is everywhere and consists of a continuous field accelerating into objects. Accelerated space = mass. The higher the acceleration, the more the mass increases. Objects do not have distinct edges. The edges taper off to where the magnitude of the mass is small and undetectable. Outer space has relatively small accelerations, but it still has some mass, although much too small for scientists to detect and measure.

The earth does not move through an independent volume of space. As the earth moves, space flows down through the earth's surface and is measured as the force of gravity. Michelson and Morley's results failed because they based their experiment on the false assumption that the earth moves through static aether instead of accelerating space flowing into the earth.

As space flows from the larger volume of outer space into the smaller volume of an object in space, the volumetric flow velocity must increase (accelerate). This acceleration of space is mass. The higher the acceleration, the larger the mass. As space continues its downward flow into the interior of an object, the flow is divided into smaller and smaller flow streams until it finally reaches the world of the atom.

At the surface of the atom, the space acceleration is so high and the volume is so low that space becomes dense enough to be detected as solid particles. Density equals mass divided by volume. In the macro world, accelerated space is gravitational force. In the micro world, accelerated space is electromagnetic force. In the sub-atomic world, accelerated space is nuclear force. Gravitational force, electromagnetic force, and the nuclear forces are different aspects of the same phenomenon of accelerated space.

The seemingly separate forces of nature are connected by the same accelerated flow of space as it moves downward from macro to micro space to sub-atomic and even potentially further. Future scientists will continue to find more forces as they develop better instruments and discover space flowing deeper and deeper into God's physical from nonphysical process.

The Space-Time Universe

Volumetric flow rate (Q) = distance^3/time

Mass (m) = distance^3/time^2

Electric charge (q) = distance^3/time

    (Electric charge is equivalent to volumetric flow)

One coulomb of electrical charge = 3.4 x 10^5 meter^3/sec

Electric current (I) = *distance^3/time^2* = *dQ/dt* = *mass*

    (Electric current is equivalent to mass.)

Density (D) = 1/time^2

Pressure (p) = distance^2/time^4

Force (F) = distance^4/time^4

Planck's constant (h) = distance^5/time^3

Energy (E) = distance^5/time^4

Voltage (V) = distance^2/time^3

Power (P) = distance^5/time^5

CHAPTER TEN

God, Providence, and Heaven

S tarting with Aristotle, Western science has been constrained by a self-imposed, freestanding paradigm. If scientists can't detect and measure it, then as far as they are concerned it doesn't exist, so they believe this physical world is all there is.

The scientific evidence does not support the modern scientific world-view. The evidence actually proves our physical universe is connected to our minds and souls. There is vastly more to the human experience than science can measure—not in our sensed measurable world but in the greater not-in-this-space-and-time world. If you believe in the modern scientific model, you will not reach your potential as a human being and your life will be minimized or even tragic.

This book has proven that modern scientists are wrong when they say they know how the universe came into existence and that a Supreme Being was not responsible. The fact is, the material world in which we live cannot be shown to exist without greater help, because scientists cannot show how matter can exist freestanding in space and time. A purely physical thing is not even scientifically possible, so there is no other scientific answer except that a Supreme Being beyond this sensed world caused it to exist and is causing it to continue to exist, or our world would cease to exist.

Today's modern scientific wrongheadedness is not a small thing. Science's strong influence has caused people to lose the greater purpose for humanity and to believe only in themselves and this life. This is a recipe for disaster, both personally and globally.

In this book I have used virtual reality as a crude analogy, because it is part of modern scientific technology and something anyone can personally experience and understand. Hopefully, virtual reality helps us to see that we live in the world in which our soul senses and interacts. You are your soul, and you are not stuck in your earthly body, as modern science claims. You live in universe proposal number two, which gives you the power to live in another world in another place.

My personal experience with other worlds goes back long before the invention of modern-day virtual reality. Beginning when I was around six years old, I learned that I could create a seemingly real world in my mind. This was not a dream. I knew what dreams were. I dreamed and still dream, like everyone else does, during sleep.

At first, my inner worlds were carefully planned and constructed by my own design. I could create and control everything. As a small child I had childish wants, so I sometimes would insert myself into a gigantic toy store, and at other times I would play the hero in my very own real world action. I was able to create in my own mind what I wanted in my outside world but could not have. This was not a day-dream world—it was a working physical reality.

The amazing thing about my inner life is that it was so vivid and life-like that I could not tell any difference between it and my real outside life. It was as real as the one you are experiencing around yourself right now. It was the same to me as living in my outer world but even better. I wondered how such a complicated and solid world could wholly exist in my mind.

The following is an account of my inner world experiences as a child. I would find a quiet place, so I could completely block out my outer reality. In this way I could completely focus on the black void of my viewing screen. After intense concentration, points of light would appear and then expand into swirling (accelerating) space. I discovered I had the power to focus on the swirling space and transform it into the complex solid world of matter that I wanted to exist in. Then I would immerse myself into my new reality. I became an active participant in a new physical world.

These inner realities disappeared as quickly as I created them when my concentration was broken from the outside, so I always had to start over from the beginning. They were temporary escapes from my real world. I realized they were in my mind and completely contained within me.

After a while my temporary worlds became routine, and I went further into my inner unknown—but not intentionally at first. I think it just happened as a result of my increasing success at disconnecting from my outer world and more intensely focusing inward. It started unexpectedly. With more powerful concentration, a hole opened up in the swirling matter and I was pulled down into it, as if falling into a well. I didn't feel afraid as I fell downward.

After some distance in darkness a faint light appeared and then grew brighter as I approached the bottom. Suddenly I found myself in the light of a new reality not of my design. It was waiting for me. I often repeated this journey to my new universe but could never stay for more than a few minutes before being brought back to my outer reality. These first deep inner experiences were as a child, and I found myself in beautiful country places.

The well transformed into a tunnel as I grew into my teen years. Unlike my childhood journeys down the well, it took intense and focused concentration to go into and all the way through the tunnel. At times my focus would be broken, and I would find myself back in my outer reality. When I did make it all the way to the end of the tunnel, my first impression was not much different than I would expect when visiting a new place in my outer world, except I felt like a temporary explorer—not a permanent resident.

My tunnel universe was always a different place but usually an unfamiliar city filled with strangers. I wouldn't know where I was going until I got there. I never met anyone that I knew from my real outer life. Looking back, I now think this was because I was still young and I had not yet set any kind of direction for myself. I had no strong ideas about life. My life was in flux. I did not know what I wanted or where I was headed, so my world at the end of the tunnel was changing as I was changing in my real world. I still feel as though it is a world that reflects my thoughts and beliefs.

My ability to visit my tunnel world began to diminish when I grew into an adult with adult responsibilities. I found it nearly impossible to disconnect from the outer world. There were people depending on me, and I had so many worldly things I could not afford not to think about. I have never forgotten, however, how vivid and real those personal experiences were. I have shared them to help show the reader that our outer reality is not the only reality that a person's soul has access to.

I have thought a lot about the world at the end of the tunnel. I think this other world does not exist within me. My experience has convinced me that it exists somewhere else in another realm. I wondered what would have happened if my outer world human body had died while I was in my world at the other end of the tunnel. I believe I would have stayed and lived on in this other world in another life.

This book has proven that we live in a human-centered universe process, so living on in another life is a designed part of the continued human journey. I think we all have a tunnel to another world, but we live in a society too caught up in the here and now to discover it. I think that each person will go through his or her own tunnel when the physical body dies. He or she will go to a world they have been unknowingly creating for themselves—good or bad. Or if they have personally known, loved, and talked to God and loved their fellow human beings in this life, then they will go through their tunnel and be with God in heaven. Many people that have died and have been brought back to life have reported this kind of experience.

Our universe is designed like proposal number two. We as souls are actually connected to the greater realm. We control our earthly bodies from outside our physical reality. This means that we have a direct communication with God. Many of us intuitively understand this and pray to our

Creator, but prayer is not quite the same as completely turning everything over to God.

The founding fathers of the United States believed strongly in an active God who watches over and helps people who believe. The founding fathers believed it was Providence that helped the United States become a free country and then eventually the beacon of freedom in the world. Surprisingly, the symbol of Providence is still on the U.S. dollar bill. Look at the pyramid. This probably won't last much longer, because today's scientists and most of the population no longer agree with our founding fathers. But if you don't believe in God and Providence, then you are left to your own abilities to survive in a world beyond your control.

In the human-centered universe model, it is easy to see how Providence is a part of our lives. Again, I cannot presume to know the realm of our Creator, but we and the world we live in is what He designed, so we would probably design our virtual worlds in a like manner, except obviously vastly less sophisticated. So, I will again use the virtual reality analogy to present an idea of how our reality works.

The virtual world and the people in it are generated by the underlying program, which was designed by a being (creator) that exists outside the reality. The active participants in the reality have programmed capabilities that would cause predetermined paths if it were not for the souls that control their virtual bodies also from outside the space and time of the virtual reality. This is how free will takes place, which makes the future of the reality undetermined. Each and every one of the people in the reality are connected to the greater realm of the Creator.

People who do have faith in God pray and believe their prayers are answered. Nonbelievers would say that things would have turned out okay anyway—how can you prove God had anything to do with it?

I used to believe in the modern scientific view that we are all on our own. As a young man I thought I was capable of handling any problem or situation. Even my job as a mechanical process engineer consisted of continual problem solving. Sometimes, though, situations become too difficult for a person's abilities. When this happened to me, I finally admitted to myself that I did not have all the answers, and I asked God to give me the answers. I found that if you truly believe in Him, then He will show you the way. I did, and He did.

For me the unquestioning belief in Providence comes when you have a problem that is so difficult and overwhelming that you see there is no way of escaping disaster. You have no way out, so you ask God to fix it for you. Your belief in your connection to God is so strong that you stop trying to do what you are not capable of doing. You even stop worrying and allow an inner peace to take hold, because you know that God will take care of you. And He does. This happened to me, and God fixed it. I also realize that if I had not believed in Providence, then disaster surely would have come down on me.

The greatest leaders in American history believed in Providence. George Washington sustained bullet holes in his clothing while leading troops into battle, but he was never wounded. Washington's army was aided by unusual events that enabled it to survive and eventually defeat a far superior British army. Had Washington been killed or his army destroyed, history would be completely different.

Abraham Lincoln talked about one of the lowest points in his presidency. It was just before the battle of Gettysburg. Everything hinged on the outcome. If the Union lost, the war would be lost, and history would be completely different. Everything was on him, and he desperately needed a victory. It was an overwhelming position to be in. Lincoln recounted that he was not worried, because he put it all in God's hands. He didn't just hope for God's help; he knew that God would fix everything. Lincoln said that he had a nice evening and slept well. The next day he was informed the Union had won and Lee was in full retreat. It was the turning point that ended the slave-holding culture of the South, and America finally became a great country.

It is interesting that our greatest leaders, George Washington and Abraham Lincoln, strongly believed in Providence, but today's leaders are removing God from public life. This is unfortunate. I once thought that I was a good problem solver, but now I wonder how much better my decisions would have been had I believed in God's guiding hand earlier in life.

Providence is when divine intervention gets you through a tough situation. When you are directly involved, you feel the hand of God on your shoulder. Someone not directly involved might say you were just lucky. A miracle is somewhat different, because it is so unbelievable that it cannot be explained away as luck. Miracles are different from Providence, because a miracle requires more than God watching over you and helping you. A miracle requires God to temporarily change the laws of nature. Using the virtual analogy, the Creator would certainly have the power to alter nature but probably would do so only in rare situations, especially in this day and age when people are so unbelieving.

In a virtual world the realm of the creator and the human operators exist outside of the space and time of the virtual world. It must also be so in our real reality. The realm of God and souls is the realm from which we look into this physical world. We view our reality on our personal viewing screen. We can design machines and robots with crude brains and software that can sense, analyze, and operate in the real world. Still, machines can only act and react according to the way they are programmed. Machines do not have free-will souls with viewing screens.

Animals are more complicated and harder to understand. Animals have a brain and software built into their physical life forms, but animals act only as nature designed them to act. They act as if they are simply here without question or self-reflection. Animals do not have free-will souls with viewing screens.

It is a human universe. Only humans have souls with self-awareness and free will. The universe program operates according to specific scientific rules, so everything follows a predetermined path except for human intervention from outside the program. The soul of a human being inhabits the human life form in the way that a human participant inhabits a life form in a virtual reality. The soul is independent of the universe program. The soul is the free-will decision-maker, with the ability to change the course of the action toward an uncertain future.

Each of us is a soul. Our earthly bodies are stuck in this material reality in which we now find ourselves living, but we are not. We are currently connected to our earthly bodies, but when our bodies die we are still connected to the greater universe. The fortunes of the people that inhabit our physical reality will always prosper or decline, so it is most important how each individual interacts while here. We are here for individual redemption. Each of us should realize that the most important thing for us in this life, as Plato said, is to not degrade our souls.

The universe is a dynamic and changing place, and we humans are at the controls with or without God's help. It is our choice. Our ancient ancestors understood this, but civilization has separated us from the natural world. Modern science's imposition of a freestanding universe has led us to perceiving the material world as an independent entity, which has caused us to feel small, insignificant, and powerless. Our modern technical skills give us an unprecedented ability to modify the physical world we live in, but we no longer believe humans have souls or that a greater universe lies beyond.

If science can update itself to the modern, human-centered model, mankind can get back on the right path. We can once again believe in a greater power, put renewed emphasis on the soul of a human being, and still have the freedom to continue advancing technically in order to improve the living conditions for all people. By understanding how the universe really works, as individuals we will regain the belief that we are special beings created by God and that we have the power to push and pull our physical surroundings to mold our reality here and beyond.

We need to change our scientific model and reclaim our rightful place at the center of God's universe.

The End

ABOUT THE AUTHOR

I was born and raised in Southern Illinois in the small rural town of Salem.

I became curious about how the universe works at a young age. Ever since I can remember I have wondered how it is that I am alive and living in the world I see and experience around me. This passion has led me to study, research and eventually write this book.

I have attended several colleges and universities. I am a graduate from Washington University in St. Louis, Missouri. My engineering career consists of working as a process/research engineer for Ralston Purina and Ralcorp in St. Louis and for General Mills in Minneapolis. I am a retired Licensed Professional Engineer in the State of Illinois.

I have learned that continual questioning and intimate knowledge is required in order to understand complicated things. My expertise is in designing things, systems of things and the operation of systems. Much of my working career has been focused on understanding and solving the problems in industrial processes. This experience coupled with my passion to accumulate scientific knowledge has helped me immensely in understanding the workings of the biggest of all physical processes, which is the whole universe.

I love to travel and experience the world. My engineering career has required extensive travel, and before and after retirement my wife and I have taken many vacations throughout the United States and in foreign countries.

I am very fortunate to have had a great career and also fulfilled my goal of uncovering the secrets of the universe while having a wonderful family life at the same time. My wife and I have raised six children and enjoy spending much time with many grandchildren.

I live in Edwardsville, Illinois with my wife Mae and our dog Allie.